Q: Skills for Success

READING AND WRITING

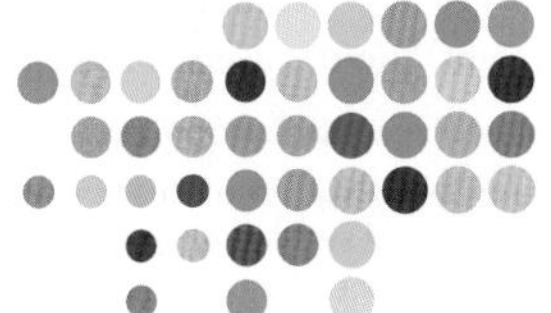

Sarah Lynn

SERIES CONSULTANTS
Marguerite Ann Snow
Lawrence J. Zwier

VOCABULARY CONSULTANT
Cheryl Boyd Zimmerman

INTENSIVE ENGLISH PROGRAM
IVC Campus

198 Madison Avenue
New York, NY 10016 USA

Great Clarendon Street, Oxford OX2 6DP UK

Oxford University Press is a department of the University of Oxford. It furthers the University's objective of excellence in research, scholarship, and education by publishing worldwide in

Oxford New York

Auckland Cape Town Dar es Salaam Hong Kong Karachi Kuala Lumpur Madrid Melbourne Mexico City Nairobi New Delhi Shanghai Taipei Toronto

With offices in

Argentina Austria Brazil Chile Czech Republic France Greece Guatemala Hungary Italy Japan Poland Portugal Singapore South Korea Switzerland Thailand Turkey Ukraine Vietnam

OXFORD and OXFORD ENGLISH are registered trademarks of Oxford University Press in certain countries.

General Manager, American ELT: Laura Pearson
Publisher: Stephanie Karras
Associate Publishing Manager: Sharon Sargent
Managing Editors: Martin Coleman, Mary Whittemore
Associate Development Editors: Rebecca Mostov, Keyana Shaw
Director, ADP: Susan Sanguily
Executive Design Manager: Maj-Britt Hagsted
Associate Design Manager: Michael Steinhofer
Electronic Production Manager: Julie Armstrong
Cover Design: Molly Scanlon
Image Manager: Trisha Masterson
Image Editors: Robin Fadool and Liaht Pashayan
Production Coordinator: Elizabeth Matsumoto

ISBN: 978-0-19-475622-8 Reading Writing 1 Student Book Pack
ISBN: 978-0-19-475638-9 Reading Writing 1 Student Book
ISBN: 978-0-19-475621-1 Q Online Practice Student Access Code Card

Printed in China

This book is printed on paper from certified and well-managed sources.

10 9 8 7 6 5

ACKNOWLEDGMENTS

The publishers would like to thank the following for their kind permission to reproduce photographs: Cover Yukmin/Asia Images/Getty Images; Jupiter Images/ Workbook Stock/Getty Images; David Anderson/iStockphoto; 4x6/ iStockphoto; Kuzma/iStockphoto; TrapdoorMedia/iStockphoto; vi Marcin Krygier/iStockphoto; xii Rüstem GÜRLER/iStockphoto; p. 2 SuperStock; p. 4 Hiep Vu/First Light/Corbis UK Ltd.; p. 7 John A. Angelillo/Corbis UK Ltd.; p. 11 FK Photo/Corbis UK Ltd.; p. 12 Christian Delbert/Shutterstock; p. 16 Banana Pancake/Alamy; p. 17 Dorling Kindersley/Getty Images; p. 21 Bruce Benedict/Transtock/Corbis UK Ltd.; p. 24 Halfdark/Getty Images; p. 26 PhotoAlto/James Hardy/Getty Images (salesclerk); p. 26 Moodboard/ Corbis UK Ltd. (construction); p. 26 Picturenet/Blend Images/Corbis UK Ltd. (driver); p. 26 Hein van den Heuvel/Cusp/Photolibrary Group (chef); p. 26 Phil Boorman/Cultura/Corbis UK Ltd. (nurse); p. 26 Red Chopsticks/ Oxford University Press (office); p. 29 DreamPictures/Shannon Faulk/Blend Images/Corbis UK Ltd. (carpenter); p. 29 Tetra Images/Corbis UK Ltd. (doctor); p. 29 Peter Titmuss/Alamy (hairdresser); p. 29 Blend Images/Oxford University Press (teacher); p. 29 Tanya Constantine/Blend Images/Corbis UK Ltd. (lawyer); p. 29 Pixland/Photolibrary Group (accountant); p. 32 Blend Images/Alamy (travel agent); p. 32 Digital Vision/Oxford University Press (nurse); p. 33 Juice Images/Corbis UK Ltd. (salesclerk); p. 33 moodboard/Alamy (web designer); p. 36 Chuck Kuhn Photography/Getty Images; p. 42 Topical Press Agency/ Hulton Archive/Getty Images; p. 46 C. Brandon/Getty Images; p. 47 Stan Kujawa/Alamy; p. 49 Digital Vision/Oxford University Press; p. 51 Asiaselects/ Corbis UK Ltd. (couple); p. 51 Hill Street Studios/Blend Images/Corbis UK Ltd. (businessman); p. 52 Jeff Greenberg/Alamy; p. 56 Photodisc/Oxford University Press; p. 60 Tetra Images/Getty Images; p. 64 Ken Seet/Corbis UK Ltd.; p. 67 DavidEnglish Photos/Alamy; p. 75 Vince Clements/Alamy; p. 78 REUTERS/ Daniel Munoz; p. 80 Gulfimages/Alamy (beach); p. 80 Jack Hollingsworth/ Corbis UK Ltd. (bridge); p. 80 Robert Harding Picture Library Ltd/Alamy (snow); p. 80 Comstock/Corbis UK Ltd. (oup_usa_Q_RW1_SBU05_05); p. 81 Photography by Ward/Alamy; p. 100 Masterfile; p. 102 Buzzshotz/Alamy (girl); p. 102 Vincent Besnault/Getty Images (boys); p. 102 Seth Resnick/ Science Faction/Corbis UK Ltd. (lobster); p. 102 Blend Images/Alamy (woman); p. 104 Zhuoming Liang/Corbis UK Ltd.; p. 109 Ned Frisk Photography/Corbis UK Ltd. (man); p. 109 moodboard/Alamy (club); p. 120 REUTERS/Nicky Loh; p. 122 Sukree Sukplang/Reuters/Corbis UK Ltd. (popular); p. 122 Blend Images/Oxford University Press (jazz); p. 122 Jeremy Hoare/Alamy (classical); p. 122 Doug Steley/Alamy (hip-hop); p. 124 Kelly Redinger/Design Pics/Corbis UK Ltd.; p. 130 Robin Smith/Photolibrary Group (violin); p. 130 Jacob Hutchings/Digital Light Source/Photolibrary Group (drum); p. 131 Lebrecht Music and Arts Photo Library/Alamy; p. 132 Ronald Grant Archive (jumping); p. 132 Hal Lieberman Company/Screen Gems/Ronald Grant Archive (spying); p. 132 Everett Collection/Rex Features (dancing); p. 140 Blend Images/ Masterfile; p. 144 Stephanie Adams/age fotostock/Photolibrary Group; p. 145 Image Source/Alamy; p. 162 SuperStock RF/SuperStock; p. 164 Beathan/ Corbis UK Ltd. (tricycle); p. 164 Ariel Skelley/Corbis UK Ltd. (salesclerk); p. 164 Sipa Press/Rex Features (skater); p. 166 David Howells/Rex Features; p. 171 Tyler Olson/Alamy; p. 172 Peter Horree/Alamy (mask); p. 172 WizData, inc./Alamy (Korean); p. 182 Ian Waldie/Getty Images spider opener; p. 184 Photoshot Holdings Ltd/Alamy (tarantula); p. 184 Richard Berenholtz/ Corbis UK Ltd. (height); p. 184 Martin Harvey/Alamy (snake); p. 184 Dlillc/ Corbis UK Ltd. (dog); p. 191 Rob Bartee/Alamy.

Illustrations by: p. 4 Claudia Carlson (ID); p. 4 Greg Paprocki (speech); p. 44 Claudia Carlson; p. 62 Jean Tuttle; p. 69 Jing Jing Tsong; p. 74 Harry Briggs; p. 142 Jean Tuttle; p. 150 Stanford Kay; p. 151 Stanford Kay; p. 164 Barb Bastian; p. 168 Karen Minot; p. 186 Karen Minot.

ACKNOWLEDGEMENTS

Author

Sarah Lynn holds an M.A. in TESOL from Teachers College, Columbia University. She has taught English to speakers of other languages for over twenty years, both in the U.S. and abroad. She leads teacher-training sessions on reading, writing, pronunciation, the multilevel classroom, study skills, collaborative learning, and cross-cultural communication. Ms. Lynn has also written numerous teacher resource books and student textbooks for English Language Learners.

Series Consultants

Marguerite Ann Snow holds a Ph.D. in Applied Linguistics from UCLA. She is a professor in the Charter College of Education at California State University, Los Angeles where she teaches in the TESOL M.A. program. She has published in *TESOL Quarterly*, *Applied Linguistics*, and *The Modern Language Journal*. She has been a Fulbright scholar in Hong Kong and Cyprus. In 2006, she received the President's Distinguished Professor award at Cal State LA. In addition to working closely with ESL and mainstream public school teachers in the U.S., she has trained EFL teachers in Algeria, Argentina, Brazil, Egypt, Japan, Morocco, Pakistan, Spain, and Turkey. Her main interests are integrated content and language instruction, English for Academic Purposes, and standards for English teaching and learning.

Lawrence J. Zwier holds an M.A. in TESL from the University of Minnesota. He is currently the Associate Director for Curriculum Development at the English Language Center at Michigan State University in East Lansing. He has taught ESL/EFL in the U.S., Saudi Arabia, Malaysia, Japan, and Singapore. He is a frequent TESOL conference presenter, and has published many ESL/EFL books in the areas of test-preparation, vocabulary, and reading, including *Inside Reading 2* for Oxford University Press.

Vocabulary Consultant

Cheryl Boyd Zimmerman is associate professor of TESOL at California State University, Fullerton. She specializes in second-language vocabulary acquisition, an area in which she is widely published. She teaches graduate courses on second-language acquisition, culture, vocabulary, and the fundamentals of TESOL, and is a frequent invited speaker on topics related to vocabulary teaching and learning. She is the author of *Word Knowledge: A Vocabulary Teacher's Handbook*, and Series Director of *Inside Reading*, both published by Oxford University Press.

REVIEWERS

We would like to acknowledge the advice of teachers from all over the world who participated in online reviews, focus groups, and editorial reviews. We relied heavily on teacher input throughout the extensive development process of the *Q* series, and many of the features in the series came directly from feedback we gathered from teachers in the classroom. We are grateful to all who helped.

UNITED STATES **Marcarena Aguilar**, North Harris College, TX; **Deborah Anholt**, Lewis and Clark College, OR; **Robert Anzelde**, Oakton Community College, IL; **Arlys Arnold**, University of Minnesota, MN; **Marcia Arthur**, Renton Technical College, WA; **Anne Bachmann**, Clackamas Community College, OR; **Ron Balsamo**, Santa Rosa Junior College, CA; **Lori Barkley**, Portland State University, OR; **Eileen Barlow**, SUNY Albany, NY; **Sue Bartch**, Cuyahoga Community College, OH; **Lora Bates**, Oakton High School, VA; **Nancy Baum**, University of Texas at Arlington, TX; **Linda Berendsen**, Oakton Community College, IL; **Jennifer Binckes Lee**, Howard Community College, MD; **Grace Bishop**, Houston Community College, TX; **Jean W. Bodman**, Union County College, NJ; **Virginia Bouchard**, George Mason University, VA; **Kimberley Briesch Sumner**, University of Southern California, CA; **Gabriela Cambiasso**, Harold Washington College, IL; **Jackie Campbell**, Capistrano Unified School District, CA; **Adele C. Camus**, George Mason University, VA; **Laura Chason**, Savannah College, GA; **Kerry Linder Catana**, Language Studies International, NY; **An Cheng**, Oklahoma State University, OK; **Carole Collins**, North Hampton Community College, PA; **Betty R. Compton**, Intercultural Communications College, HI; **Pamela Couch**, Boston University, MA; **Fernanda Crowe**, Intrax International Institute, CA; **Margo Czinski**, Washtenaw Community College, MI; **David Dahnke**, Lone Star College, TX; **Gillian M. Dale**, CA; **L. Dalgish**, Concordia College, MN; **Christopher Davis**, John Jay College, NY; **Sonia Delgadillo**, Sierra College, CA; **Marta O. Dmytrenko-Ahrabian**, Wayne State University, MI; **Javier Dominguez**, Central High School, SC; **Jo Ellen Downey-Greer**, Lansing Community College, MI; **Jennifer Duclos**, Boston University, MA; **Yvonne Duncan**, City College of San Francisco, CA; **Jennie Farnell**, University of Connecticut, CT; **Susan Fedors**, Howard Community College, MD; **Matthew Florence**, Intrax International Institute, CA; **Kathleen Flynn**, Glendale College, CA; **Eve Fonseca**, St. Louis Community College, MO; **Elizabeth Foss**, Washtenaw Community College, MI; **Duff C. Galda**, Pima Community College, AZ; **Christiane Galvani**, Houston Community College, TX; **Gretchen Gerber**, Howard Community College, MD; **Ray Gonzalez**, Montgomery College, MD; **Alyona Gorokhova**, Grossmont College, CA; **John Graney**, Santa Fe College, FL; **Kathleen Green**, Central High School, AZ; **Webb Hamilton**, De Anza College, San Jose City College, CA; **Janet Harclerode**, Santa Monica Community College, CA; **Sandra Hartmann**, Language and Culture Center, TX; **Kathy Haven**, Mission College, CA; **Adam Henricksen**, University of Maryland, MD; **Peter Hoffman**, LaGuardia Community College, NY; **Linda Holden**, College of Lake County, IL; **Jana Holt**, Lake Washington Technical College, WA; **Gail Ibele**, University of Wisconsin, WI; **Mandy Kama**, Georgetown University, Washington, DC; **Stephanie Kasuboski**, Cuyahoga Community College, OH; **Chigusa Katoku**, Mission College, CA; **Sandra Kawamura**, Sacramento City College, CA; **Gail Kellersberger**, University of Houston-Downtown, TX; **Jane Kelly**, Durham Technical Community College, NC; **Julie Park Kim**, George Mason University, VA; **Lisa Kovacs-Morgan** University of California, San Diego, CA; **Claudia Kupiec**, DePaul University, IL; **Renee La Rue**, Lone Star College-Montgomery, TX; **Janet Langon**, Glendale College, CA; **Lawrence Lawson**, Palomar College, CA; **Rachele Lawton**, The Community College of Baltimore County, MD; **Alice Lee**, Richland College, TX; **Cherie Lenz-Hackett**, University of Washington, WA; **Joy Leventhal**, Cuyahoga Community College, OH; **Candace Lynch-Thompson**, North Orange County Community College District, CA; **Thi Thi Ma**, City College of San Francisco, CA; **Denise Maduli-Williams**, City College of San Francisco, CA; **Eileen Mahoney**, Camelback High School, AZ; **Brigitte Maronde**, Harold Washington College, IL; **Keith Maurice**, University of Texas at Arlington, TX; **Nancy Mayer**, University of Missouri-St. Louis, MO; **Karen Merritt**, Glendale Union High School District, AZ; **Holly Milkowart**, Johnson County Community College, KS; **Eric Moyer**, Intrax International Institute, CA; **Gino Muzzatti**, Santa Rosa Junior College, CA; **William Nedrow**, Triton College, IL; **Eric Nelson**, University of Minnesota, MN; **Rhony Ory**, Ygnacio Valley High School, CA; **Paul Parent**, Montgomery College, MD; **Oscar Pedroso**, Miami Dade College, FL; **Robin Persiani**, Sierra College, CA; **Patricia Prenz-Belkin**, Hostos Community College, NY; **Jim Ranalli**, Iowa State University, IA; **Toni R. Randall**, Santa Monica College, CA; **Vidya Rangachari**, Mission College, CA; **Elizabeth Rasmussen**, Northern Virginia Community College, VA; **Lara Ravitch**, Truman College, IL; **Deborah Repasz**, San Jacinto College, TX; **Andrey Reznikov**, Black Hills State University, SD; **Alison Rice**, Hunter College, NY; **Jennifer Robles**, Ventura Unified School District, CA; **Priscilla Rocha**, Clark County School District, NV; **Dzidra Rodins**, DePaul University IL; **Maria Rodriguez**, Central High School, AZ; **Maria Ruiz**, Victor Valley College, CA; **Kimberly Russell**, Clark College, WA; **Irene Sakk**, Northwestern University, IL; **Shaeley Santiago**, Ames High School, IA; **Peg Sarosy**, San Francisco State University, CA; **Alice Savage**, North Harris College, TX; **Donna Schaeffer**, University of Washington, WA; **Carol Schinger**, Northern Virginia Community College, VA; **Robert Scott**, Kansas State University, KS; **Suell Scott**, Sheridan Technical Center, FL; **Shira Seaman**, Global English Academy, NY; **Richard Seltzer**, Glendale Community College, CA; **Kathy Sherak**, San Francisco State University, CA; **German Silva**, Miami Dade College, FL; **Andrea Spector**, Santa Monica Community College, CA; **Karen Stanely**, Central Piedmont Community College, NC; **Ayse Stromsdorfer**, Soldan I.S.H.S., MO; **Yilin Sun**, South Seattle Community College, WA; **Thomas Swietlik**, Intrax International Institute, IL; **Judith Tanka**, UCLA Extension–American Language Center, CA; **Priscilla Taylor**, University of Southern California, CA; **Ilene Teixeira**, Fairfax County Public Schools, VA; **Shirl H. Terrell**, Collin College, TX; **Marya Teutsch-Dwyer**, St. Cloud State University, MN; **Stephen Thergesen**, ELS Language Centers, CO; **Christine Tierney**, Houston Community College, TX; **Arlene Turini**, North Moore High School, NC; **Suzanne Van Der Valk**, Iowa State University, IA; **Nathan D. Vasarhely**, Ygnacio Valley High School, CA; **Naomi S. Verratti**, Howard Community College, MD; **Hollyahna Vettori**, Santa Rosa Junior College, CA; **Julie Vorholt**, Lewis & Clark College, OR; **Laura Walsh**, City College of San Francisco, CA; **Andrew J. Watson**, The English Bakery; **Donald Weasenforth**, Collin College, TX; **Juliane Widner**, Sheepshead Bay High School, NY; **Lynne Wilkins**, Mills College, CA; **Dolores "Lorrie" Winter**, California State University at Fullerton, CA; **Jody Yamamoto**, Kapi'olani Community College, HI; **Ellen L. Yaniv**, Boston University, MA; **Norman Yoshida**, Lewis & Clark College, OR; **Joanna Zadra**, American River College, CA; **Florence Zysman**, Santiago Canyon College, CA;

ASIA **Rabiatu Abubakar**, Eton Language Centre, Malaysia; **Wiwik Andreani**, Bina Nusantara University, Indonesia; **Mike Baker**, Kosei Junior High School, Japan; **Leonard Barrow**, Kanto Junior College, Japan; **Herman Bartelen**, Japan; **Siren Betty**, Fooyin University, Kaohsiung; **Thomas E. Bieri**, Nagoya College, Japan; **Natalie Brezden**, Global English House, Japan; **MK Brooks**, Mukogawa Women's University, Japan; **Truong Ngoc Buu**, The Youth Language School, Vietnam; **Charles Cabell**, Toyo University, Japan; **Fred Carruth**, Matsumoto University, Japan; **Frances Causer**, Seijo University, Japan; **Deborah Chang**, Wenzao Ursuline College of Languages, Kaohsiung; **David Chatham**, Ritsumeikan University, Japan; **Andrew Chih Hong Chen**, National Sun Yat-sen University, Kaohsiung; **Christina Chen**, Yu-Tsai Bilingual Elementary School, Taipei; **Jason Jeffree Cole**, Coto College, Japan; **Le Minh Cong**, Vungtau Tourism Vocational College, Vietnam; **Todd Cooper**, Toyama National College of Technology, Japan; **Marie Cosgrove**, Daito Bunka University, Japan; **Tony Cripps**, Ritsumeikan University, Japan; **Daniel Cussen**, Takushoku University, Japan; **Le Dan**, Ho Chi Minh City Electric Power College, Vietnam; **Simon Daykin**, Banghwa-dong Community Centre, South Korea; **Aimee Denham**, ILA, Vietnam; **Bryan Dickson**, David's English Center, Taipei; **Nathan Ducker**, Japan University, Japan; **Ian Duncan**, Simul International Corporate Training, Japan; **Nguyen Thi Kieu Dung**, Thang Long University, Vietnam; **Nguyen Thi Thuy Duong**, Vietnamese American Vocational Training College, Vietnam; **Wong Tuck Ee**, Raja Tun Azlan Science Secondary School, Malaysia; **Emilia Effendy**, International Islamic University Malaysia, Malaysia; **Robert Eva**, Kaisei Girls High School, Japan; **Jim George**, Luna International Language School, Japan; **Jurgen Germeys**, Silk Road Language Center, South Korea; **Wong Ai Gnoh**, SMJK

Chung Hwa Confucian, Malaysia; **Peter Goosselink**, Hokkai High School, Japan; **Wendy M. Gough**, St. Mary College/Nunoike Gaigo Senmon Gakko, Japan; **Tim Grose**, Sapporo Gakuin University, Japan; **Pham Thu Ha**, Le Van Tam Primary School, Vietnam; **Ann-Marie Hadzima**, Taipei; **Troy Hammond**, Tokyo Gakugei University International Secondary School, Japan; **Robiatul 'Adawiah Binti Hamzah**, SMK Putrajaya Precinct 8(1), Malaysia; **Tran Thi Thuy Hang**, Ho Chi Minh City Banking University, Vietnam; **To Thi Hong Hanh**, CEFALT, Vietnam; **Janis Hearn**, Hongik University, South Korea; **David Hindman**, Sejong University, South Korea; **Nahn Cam Hoa**, Ho Chi Minh City University of Technology, Vietnam; **Jana Holt**, Korea University, South Korea; **Jason Hollowell**, Nihon University, Japan; **F. N. (Zoe) Hsu**, National Tainan University, Yong Kang; **Wenhua Hsu**, I-Shou University, Kaohsiung; **Luu Nguyen Quoc Hung,** Cantho University, Vietnam ; **Cecile Hwang**, Changwon National University, South Korea; **Ainol Haryati Ibrahim**, Universiti Malaysia Pahang, Malaysia; **Robert Jeens**, Yonsei University, South Korea; **Linda M. Joyce**, Kyushu Sangyo University, Japan; **Dr. Nisai Kaewsanchai**, English Square Kanchanaburi, Thailand; **Aniza Kamarulzaman**, Sabah Science Secondary School, Malaysia; **Ikuko Kashiwabara**, Osaka Electro-Communication University, Japan; **Gurmit Kaur**, INTI College, Malaysia; **Nick Keane**, Japan; **Ward Ketcheson,** Aomori University, Japan; **Montchatry Ketmuni**, Rajamangala University of Technology, Thailand; **Dinh Viet Khanh**, Vietnam; **Seonok Kim**, Kangsu Jongro Language School, South Korea; **Kelly P. Kimura**, Soka University, Japan; **Stan Kirk**, Konan University, Japan; **Donald Knight**, Nan Hua/Fu Li Junior High Schools, Hsinchu; **Kari J. Kostiainen**, Nagoya City University, Japan; **Pattri Kuanpulpol**, Silpakorn University, Thailand; **Ha Thi Lan**, Thai Binh Teacher Training College, Vietnam; **Eric Edwin Larson**, Miyazaki Prefectural Nursing University, Japan; **Richard S. Lavin**, Prefectural University of Kumamoto, Japan; **Shirley Leane**, Chugoku Junior College, Japan; **Tae Lee**, Yonsei University, South Korea; **Lys Yongsoon Lee**, Reading Town Geumcheon, South Korea; **Mallory Leece**, Sun Moon University, South Korea; **Dang Hong Lien**, Tan Lam Upper Secondary School, Vietnam; **Huang Li-Han**, Rebecca Education Institute, Taipei; **Sovannarith Lim**, Royal University of Phnom Penh, Cambodia; **Ginger Lin**, National Kaohsiung Hospitality College, Kaohsiung; **Noel Lineker**, New Zealand/Japan; **Tran Dang Khanh Linh**, Nha Trang Teachers' Training College, Vietnam; **Daphne Liu**, Buliton English School, Taipei; **S. F. Josephine Liu**, Tien-Mu Elementary School, Taipei ; **Caroline Luo**, Tunghai University, Taichung; **Jeng-Jia Luo**, Tunghai University, Taichung; **Laura MacGregor**, Gakushuin University, Japan; **Amir Madani**, Visuttharangsi School, Thailand; **Elena Maeda**, Sacred Heart Professional Training College, Japan; **Vu Thi Thanh Mai**, Hoang Gia Education Center, Vietnam; **Kimura Masakazu**, Kato Gakuen Gyoshu High School, Japan; **Susumu Matsuhashi**, Net Link English School, Japan; **James McCrostie**, Daito Bunka University, Japan; **Joel McKee**, Inha University, South Korea; **Colin McKenzie**, Wachirawit Primary School, Thailand; **William K. Moore**, Hiroshima Kokusai Gakuin University, Japan; **Hudson Murrell**, Baiko Gakuin University, Japan; **Frances Namba**, Senri International School of Kwansei Gakuin, Japan; **Keiichi Narita**, Niigata University, Japan; **Kim Chung Nguyen**, Ho Chi Minh University of Industry, Vietnam; **Do Thi Thanh Nhan**, Hanoi University, Vietnam; **Dale Kazuo Nishi**, Aoyama English Conversation School, Japan; **Louise Ohashi**, Shukutoku University, Japan; **Virginia Peng**, Ritsumeikan University, Japan; **Suangkanok Piboonthamnont**, Rajamangala University of Technology, Thailand; **Simon Pitcher**, Business English Teaching Services, Japan; **John C. Probert**, New Education Worldwide, Thailand; **Do Thi Hoa Quyen**, Ton Duc Thang University, Vietnam; **John P. Racine**, Dokkyo University, Japan; **Kevin Ramsden**, Kyoto University of Foreign Studies, Japan; **Luis Rappaport**, Cung Thieu Nha Ha Noi, Vietnam; **Lisa Reshad**, Konan Daigaku Hyogo, Japan; **Peter Riley**, Taisho University, Japan; **Thomas N. Robb**, Kyoto Sangyo University, Japan; **Maria Feti Rosyani,** Universitas Kristen Indonesia, Indonesia; **Greg Rouault**, Konan University, Japan; **Chris Ruddenklau**, Kindai University, Japan; **Hans-Gustav Schwartz**, Thailand; **Mary-Jane Scott**, Soongsil University, South Korea; **Jenay Seymour,** Hongik University, South Korea; **James Sherlock**, A.P.W. Angthong, Thailand; **Yuko Shimizu**, Ritsumeikan University, Japan; **Suzila Mohd Shukor**, Universiti Sains Malaysia, Malaysia; **Stephen E. Smith**, Mahidol University, Thailand; **Mi-young Song**, Kyungwon University, South Korea; **Jason Stewart**, Taejon International Language School, South Korea; **Brian A. Stokes,** Korea University, South Korea; **Mulder Su**, Shih-Chien University, Kaohsiung; **Yoomi Suh**, English Plus, South Korea; **Yun-Fang Sun**, Wenzao Ursuline College of Languages, Kaohsiung; **Richard Swingle**, Kansai Gaidai University, Japan; **Tran Hoang Tan**, School of International Training, Vietnam; **Takako Tanaka**, Doshisha University, Japan; **Jeffrey Taschner**, American University Alumni Language Center, Thailand ; **Michael Taylor**, International Pioneers School, Thailand; **Tran Duong The**, Sao Mai Language Center, Vietnam; **Tran Dinh Tho**, Duc Tri Secondary School, Vietnam; **Huynh Thi Anh Thu**, Nhatrang College of Culture Arts and Tourism, Vietnam; **Peter Timmins**, Peter's English School, Japan; **Fumie Togano**, Hosei Daini High School, Japan; **F. Sigmund Topor**, Keio University Language School, Japan; **Yen-Cheng Tseng**, Chang-Jung Christian University, Tainan; **Hajime Uematsu**, Hirosaki University, Japan; **Rachel Um**, Mok-dong Oedae English School, South Korea; **David Underhill**, EEExpress, Japan; **Siriluck Usaha**, Sripatum University, Thailand; **Tyas Budi Utami**, Indonesia; **Nguyen Thi Van**, Far East International School, Vietnam; **Stephan Van Eycken**, Kosei Gakuen Girls High School, Japan; **Zisa Velasquez**, Taihu International School/Semarang International School, China/Indonesia; **Jeffery Walter**, Sangji University, South Korea; **Bill White**, Kinki University, Japan; **Yohanes De Deo Widyastoko**, Xaverius Senior High School, Indonesia; **Greg Chung-Hsien Wu**, Providence University, Taichung; **Hui-Lien Yeh**, Chai Nan University of Pharmacy and Science, Tainan; **Sittiporn Yodnil**, Huachiew Chalermprakiet University, Thailand; **Shamshul Helmy Zambahari**, Universiti Teknologi Malaysia, Malaysia; **Ming-Yuli**, Chang Jung Christian University, Tainan; **Aimin Fadhlee bin Mahmud Zuhodi**, Kuala Terengganu Science School, Malaysia;

TURKEY **Gül Akkoç**, Boğaziçi University; **Seval Akmeşe**, Haliç University; **Deniz Balım**, Haliç University; **Robert Ledbury**, Izmir University of Economics; **Oya Özağaç**, Boğaziçi University;

THE MIDDLE EAST **Amina Saif Mohammed Al Hashamia**, Nizwa College of Applied Sciences, Oman; **Sharon Ruth Devaneson**, Ibri College of Technology, Oman; **Hanaa El-Deeb**, Canadian International College, Egypt; **Brian Gay**, Sultan Qaboos University, Oman; **Gail Al-Hafidh**, Sharjah Higher Colleges of Technology, U.A.E.; **Jonathan Hastings**, American Language Center, Jordan; **Sian Khoury**, Fujairah Women's College (HCT), U.A.E.; **Jessica March**, American University of Sharjah, U.A.E.; **Neil McBeath**, Sultan Qaboos University, Oman;

LATIN AMERICA **Aldana Aguirre**, Argentina; **Claudia Almeida**, Coordenação de Idiomas, Brazil; **Cláudia Arias**, Brazil; **Maria de los Angeles Barba**, FES Acatlan UNAM, Mexico; **Lilia Barrios**, Universidad Autónoma de Tamaulipas, Mexico; **Adán Beristain**, UAEM, Mexico; **Ricardo Böck**, Manoel Ribas, Brazil; **Edson Braga**, CNA, Brazil; **Marli Buttelli**, Mater et Magistra, Brazil; **Alessandra Campos**, Inova Centro de Linguas, Brazil; **Priscila Catta Preta Ribeiro**, Brazil; **Gustavo Cestari**, Access International School, Brazil; **Walter D'Alessandro**, Virginia Language Center, Brazil; **Lilian De Gennaro**, Argentina; **Mônica De Stefani**, Quality Centro de Idiomas, Brazil; **Julio Alejandro Flores**, BUAP, Mexico; **Mirian Freire**, CNA Vila Guilherme, Brazil; **Francisco Garcia**, Colegio Lestonnac de San Angel, Mexico; **Miriam Giovanardi**, Brazil; **Darlene Gonzalez Miy**, ITESM CCV, Mexico; **Maria Laura Grimaldi**, Argentina; **Luz Dary Guzmán**, IMPAHU, Colombia; **Carmen Koppe**, Brazil; **Monica Krutzler**, Brazil; **Marcus Murilo Lacerda**, Seven Idiomas, Brazil; **Nancy Lake**, CEL-LEP, Brazil; **Cris Lazzerini**, Brazil; **Sandra Luna**, Argentina; **Ricardo Luvisan**, Brazil; **Jorge Murilo Menezes**, ACBEU, Brazil; **Monica Navarro**, Instituto Cultural A. C., Mexico; **Joacyr Oliveira**, Faculdades Metropolitanas Unidas and Summit School for Teachers, Brazil; **Ayrton Cesar Oliveira de Araujo**, E&A English Classes, Brazil; **Ana Laura Oriente**, Seven Idiomas, Brazil; **Adelia Peña Clavel**, CELE UNAM, Mexico; **Beatriz Pereira**, Summit School, Brazil; **Miguel Perez**, Instituto Cultural Mexico; **Cristiane Perone**, Associação Cultura Inglesa, Brazil; **Pamela Claudia Pogré**, Colegio Integral Caballito / Universidad de Flores, Argentina; **Dalva Prates**, Brazil; **Marianne Rampaso**, Iowa Idiomas, Brazil; **Daniela Rutolo**, Instituto Superior Cultural Británico, Argentina; **Maione Sampaio**, Maione Carrijo Consultoria em Inglês Ltda, Brazil; **Elaine Santesso**, TS Escola de Idiomas, Brazil; **Camila Francisco Santos**, UNS Idiomas, Brazil; **Lucia Silva**, Cooplem Idiomas, Brazil; **Maria Adela Sorzio**, Instituto Superior Santa Cecilia, Argentina; **Elcio Souza**, Unibero, Brazil; **Willie Thomas**, Rainbw Idiomas, Brazil; **Sandra Villegas**, Instituto Humberto de Paolis, Argentina; **John Whelan**, La Universidad Nacional Autonoma de Mexico, Mexico

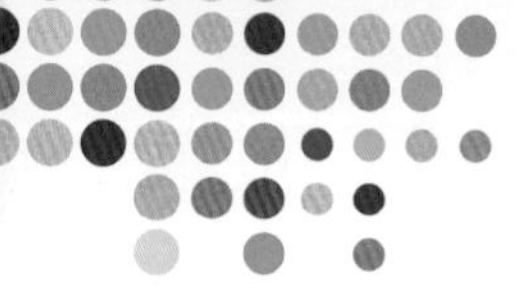

WELCOME TO Q: Skills for Success

Q: Skills for Success is a six-level series with two strands, *Reading and Writing* and *Listening and Speaking*.

READING AND WRITING

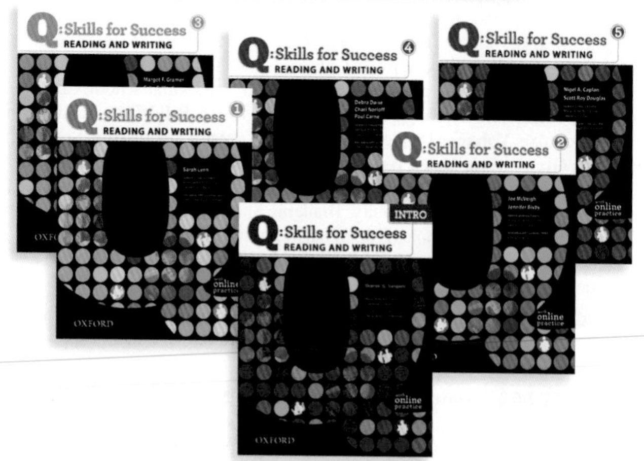

LISTENING AND SPEAKING

WITH Q ONLINE PRACTICE

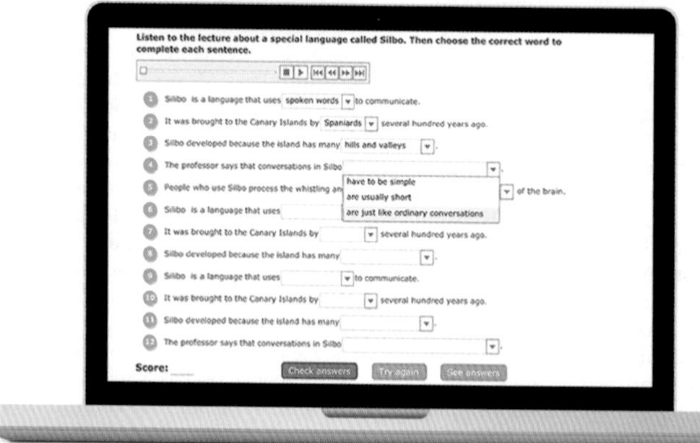

STUDENT AND TEACHER INFORMED

Q: Skills for Success is the result of an extensive development process involving thousands of teachers and hundreds of students around the world. Their views and opinions helped shape the content of the series. *Q* is grounded in teaching theory as well as real-world classroom practice, making it the most learner-centered series available.

CONTENTS

Q connects critical thinking, language skills, and learning outcomes.

QUICK GUIDE

LANGUAGE SKILLS

Explicit skills instruction enables students to meet their academic and professional goals.

LEARNING OUTCOMES

Clearly identified **learning outcomes** focus students on the goal of their instruction.

UNIT 6

Laughter

READING identifying the topic sentence in a paragraph
VOCABULARY using the dictionary
GRAMMAR sentences with *when*
WRITING writing a topic sentence

LEARNING OUTCOME

Explain what makes you or someone you know laugh.

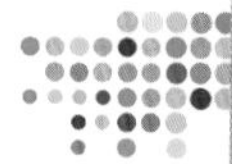

Unit QUESTION

What makes you laugh?

PREVIEW THE UNIT

A **Discuss these questions with your classmates.**

Do you laugh often?

What kind of laugh do you have? Is it loud or quiet?

Look at the photo. Why are the women laughing?

B **Discuss the Unit Question above with your classmates.**

Listen to *The Q Classroom*, Track 2 on CD 2, to hear other answers.

100 UNIT 6

101

CRITICAL THINKING

Thought-provoking **unit questions** engage students with the topic and provide a **critical thinking framework** for the unit.

Having the learning outcome is important because it gives students and teachers a clear idea of what the point of each task/activity in the unit is.

Lawrence Lawson, Palomar College, California

LANGUAGE SKILLS

Two reading texts provide input on the unit question and give **exposure to academic content.**

The Best Medicine Is Laughter

Reasons to Laugh

1 Laughter is good exercise. It makes you **breathe** quickly. Laughter makes your heart **rate** go up, and it can turn your face red. Laughter can even make you **cry**! Ten to fifteen minutes of laughing burns 50 calories[1]. It exercises your whole body.

2 Laughter has a positive **effect** on your health. It reduces high blood pressure[2] and can **prevent** some illnesses. Also,

CRITICAL THINKING

Students **discuss** their opinions of each reading text and **analyze** how it changes their perspective on the unit question.

What Do You Think?

A. Complete the activities in a group.

1. What happens to you when you laugh for a long time? How do you feel after you laugh? Use ideas from the box or your own ideas.

breathe deeply	cry	heart rate increases
breathe quickly	face turns red	stomach hurts

B. Think about both Reading 1 and Reading 2 as you discuss the questions.

1. How can you get more laughter into your life?
2. Is it important for a person to have a sense of humor? Why or why not?

One of the best features is your focus on developing materials of a high "interest level."

Troy Hammond, Tokyo Gakugei University, International Secondary School, Japan

QUICK GUIDE

Explicit skills instruction prepares students for academic success.

LANGUAGE SKILLS

Explicit instruction and practice in reading, vocabulary, grammar and writing skills **help students achieve language proficiency.**

LEARNING OUTCOMES

Practice activities allow students to **master the skills** before they are evaluated at the end of the unit.

WHAT DO YOU THINK?

Ask and answer the questions with a partner. Then choose one question and write two to three sentences about it in your notebook.

1. Ask and answer the questions in the chart. Check (✓) your partner's answers. Add one more question to the chart.

Do you laugh . . .	Never	Sometimes	Often
1. . . . when you are nervous?	☐	☐	☐
2. . . . when you hear a joke?	☐	☐	☐
3. . . . when you hear other people laugh?	☐	☐	☐
4. . . . when you are embarrassed?	☐	☐	☐
5. . . . when something surprises you?	☐	☐	☐
6. . . . when ______________?	☐	☐	☐

2. Who are you with when you laugh a lot? Where are you? What are you doing?

Reading Skill Identifying the topic sentence in a paragraph (web)

The **topic sentence** explains the main idea of a paragraph. Other sentences in a paragraph support the topic sentence. Often, the topic sentence is the first sentence of a paragraph, but sometimes it is the second or third sentence. Finding the topic sentence helps you quickly understand what the paragraph is about.

Robert Provine studied people and laughter. **He discovered that people laugh when they want to be friendly.** He watched people in the city walking and shopping. He found that 80 to 90 percent of laughter came after sentences like *I know* or *I'll see you later.* People didn't laugh because someone said something funny. People laughed because they wanted to be friendly with each other.

106 UNIT 6 | What makes you laugh?

WRITING

Grammar Sentences with *when* (web)

You can combine two sentences with *when. When* introduces a situation or state, and it means that anytime that situation or state happens, something else happens.

- There is a comma if the sentence begins with *when.* There is no comma if *when* is in the middle of the sentence.
- When the subject in both sentences is the same, use a pronoun in the second part of the sentence.

They are nervous. → They laugh.	Bob laughs. → He feels less stress.
When they are nervous, they laugh.	**When** Bob laughs, he feels less stress.
They laugh **when** they are nervous.	Bob feels less stress **when** he laughs.

A. Write two sentences with *when*. Remember that *when* introduces the situation or state that causes another situation or state.

1. I go out with my friends. → I laugh a lot.
   a. When I go out with my friends, I laugh a lot.
   b. I laugh a lot when I go out with my friends.
2. You laugh. → Your blood pressure goes down.
   a. ______________
   b. ______________
3. He sees something funny. → He laughs.
   a. ______________
   b. ______________
4. You laugh. → You use calories.
   a. ______________
   b. ______________

| Reading and Writing 113

The tasks are simple, accessible, user-friendly, and very useful.
Jessica March, American University of Sharjah, U.A.E.

LEARNER CENTERED

Q Online Practice provides all new content for additional practice in an easy-to-use online workbook. Every student book includes a ***Q Online Practice access code card***. Use the access code to register for your *Q Online Practice* account at www.Qonlinepractice.com.

Vocabulary Skill Using the dictionary 

When you see a word you don't know in a text, it helps to **identify the part of speech** of the word. *Nouns, verbs, adjectives*, and *adverbs* are examples of parts of speech. Knowing the part of speech helps you better understand the meaning and use of the word. If you aren't sure, you can find the part of speech for the vocabulary words in this book on the last page of each unit (in *Track Your Success*). You can also find the part of speech in a dictionary.

laugh[1] /læf/ *verb* (laughs, laugh·ing, laughed)
to make sounds to show that you are happy or that you think something is funny: *His jokes always make me laugh.*

laugh[2] /læf/ *noun* [*count*]
the sound you make when you are happy or when you think something is funny: *My brother has a loud laugh.* • *She told us a joke and we all* ***had a good laugh*** (= laughed a lot).

All dictionary entries are taken from the *Oxford American Dictionary for learners of English*.

LANGUAGE SKILLS

A **research-based vocabulary program** focuses students on the words they need to know academically and professionally, using skill strategies based on the same research as the Oxford dictionaries.

Your key to building English language skills NEW

Oxford Basic AMERICAN DICTIONARY for learners of English

with interactive dictionary on CD-ROM

All dictionary entries are taken from the *Oxford Basic American Dictionary for learners of English*.

The ***Oxford American Dictionary for learners of English*** was designed with English learners in mind, and provides extra learning tools for pronunciation, verb types, basic grammar structures, and more.

The Oxford 2000 Keywords

The Oxford 2000 keywords encompasses the 2000 most important words to learn in English. It is based on a comprehensive analysis of the Oxford English Corpus, a two billion word collection of English text, and on extensive research with both language and pedagogical experts.

The Academic Word List AWL

The Academic Word List was created by Averil Coxhead and contains **570 words that are commonly used in academic English**, such as in textbooks or articles across a wide range of academic subject areas. These words are a great place to start if you are studying English for academic purposes.

QUICK GUIDE

Clear learning outcomes focus students on the goals of instruction.

LEARNING OUTCOMES

A culminating unit assignment evaluates the students' **mastery of the learning outcome.**

Unit Assignment | **Write a paragraph about what makes someone laugh**

In this assignment, you are going to write a paragraph explaining what makes you or someone you know laugh. As you prepare your paragraph, think about the Unit Question, "What makes you laugh?" and refer to the Self-Assessment checklist on page 118.

For alternative unit assignments, see the *Q: Skills for Success Teacher's Handbook*.

PLAN AND WRITE

A. BRAINSTORM Think of situations that make you or someone you know laugh. Complete the chart with three situations for each type of laughter. Use vocabulary from the unit when you can.

Type of Laughter	Situations That Make You or Someone You Know Laugh
Nervous or embarrassed	**1.** **2.** **3.**
Something is funny	**1.** **2.** **3.**
Want to be friendly	**1.** **2.** **3.**

LEARNER CENTERED

Track Your Success allows students to **assess their own progress** and provides guidance on remediation.

Check (✓) the skills you learned. If you need more work on a skill, refer to the page(s) in parentheses.

READING	I can identify the topic sentence in a paragraph. (p. 106)
VOCABULARY	I can identify parts of speech in the dictionary. (p. 111)
GRAMMAR	I can recognize and use sentences with *when*. (p. 113)
WRITING	I can write a topic sentence. (p. 114)
LEARNING OUTCOME	I can explain what makes me or someone I know laugh.

Students can check their learning . . . and they can focus on the essential points when they study.

Suh Yoomi, Seoul, South Korea

Q Online Practice

For the student

- **Easy-to-use:** a simple interface allows students to focus on enhancing their reading and writing skills, not learning a new software program
- **Flexible:** for use anywhere there's an Internet connection
- **Access code card:** a *Q Online Practice* access code is included with this book—use the access code to register for *Q Online Practice* at www.Qonlinepractice.com

For the teacher

- **Simple yet powerful:** automatically grades student exercises and tracks progress
- **Straightforward:** online management system to review, print, or export reports
- **Flexible:** for use in the classroom or easily assigned as homework
- **Access code card:** contact your sales rep for your *Q Online Practice* teacher's access code

Teacher Resources

Q Teacher's Handbook gives strategic support through:

- specific teaching notes for each activity
- ideas for ensuring student participation
- multilevel strategies and expansion activities
- the answer key
- special sections on 21st Century Skills and critical thinking
- a ***Testing Program CD-ROM*** with a customizable test for each unit

For additional resources visit the *Q: Skills for Success* companion website at www.oup.com/elt/teacher/Qskillsforsuccess

Q Class Audio includes:

- reading texts
- *The Q Classroom*

It's an interesting, engaging series which provides plenty of materials that are easy to use in class, as well as instructionally promising.

Donald Weasenforth, Collin College, Texas

SCOPE AND SEQUENCE | Reading and Writing 1

<table>
<tr><th>UNIT</th><th>READING</th><th>WRITING</th></tr>
<tr><td>1 Names
Q How did you get your name?
READING 1: Naming Around the World
A Magazine Article (Names)
READING 2: Naming the Blackberry
An Online Article (Marketing)</td><td>• Preview text
• Read for main ideas
• Read for details
• Use glosses and footnotes to aid comprehension
• Read and recognize different text types
• Use charts to aid comprehension of text
• Scan text to locate specific information</td><td>• Plan before writing
• Revise, edit, and rewrite
• Give feedback to peers and self-assess
• Identify and capitalize proper nouns to improve accuracy in writing
• Write well-formed, complete sentences using unit vocabulary and simple present tense</td></tr>
<tr><td>2 Work
Q What is a good job?
READING 1: The Right Job for You
A Web Page (Jobs and Careers)
READING 2: The World of Work
A Magazine Article (Business)</td><td>• Preview text
• Read for main ideas
• Read for details
• Use glosses and footnotes to aid comprehension
• Read and recognize different text types
• Use photos/pictures to activate schema before reading
• Read titles and headings to prepare to read
• Complete a survey to relate topic to self</td><td>• Plan before writing
• Revise, edit, and rewrite
• Give feedback to peers and self-assess
• Recognize differences between fragments and complete sentences
• Write complete sentences about the unit topic</td></tr>
<tr><td>3 Long Distance
Q Why do people immigrate to other countries?
READING 1: The World in a City
A Web Page (Immigration)
READING 2: Immigrant Stories
A Magazine Article (Sociology)</td><td>• Preview text
• Read for main ideas
• Read for details
• Use glosses and footnotes to aid comprehension
• Read and recognize different text types
• Skim for main ideas to aid comprehension of text
• Anticipate reading content by analyzing text features such as headings, pictures, and captions
• Read maps to locate selected information</td><td>• Plan before writing
• Revise, edit, and rewrite
• Give feedback to peers and self-assess
• Use conjunctions and and but to connect simple sentences
• Write sentences about the unit topic</td></tr>
<tr><td>4 Positive Thinking
Q What are the benefits of positive thinking?
READING 1: The Power of Positive Thinking?
A Magazine Article (Psychology)
READING 2: The Lost Horse
An Old Chinese Story (Literature)</td><td>• Preview text
• Read for main ideas
• Read for details
• Use glosses and footnotes to aid comprehension
• Read and recognize different text types
• Complete a quiz to gain background information on a topic
• Make inferences to understand ideas not stated directly in the text</td><td>• Plan before writing
• Revise, edit, and rewrite
• Give feedback to peers and self-assess
• Use time order words to show the sequence of events in writing
• Write a story about the unit topic</td></tr>
</table>

VOCABULARY	GRAMMAR	CRITICAL THINKING	UNIT OUTCOME
• Match definitions • Define new terms • Understand meaning from context • Use the dictionary to locate correct word spellings using alphabetical order	• Simple present: Affirmative and negative statements	• Reflect on the unit question • Connect ideas across readings • Set and achieve goals • Apply unit tips and use *Q Online Practice* to become a strategic learner • Support answers with examples and opinions • Analyze reasons behind likes and dislikes • Apply information from reading to own situation	• Write about a name that you like, giving information about the name.
• Match definitions • Define new terms • Understand meaning from context • Expand vocabulary through recognizing nouns and verbs with same forms	• Verbs + infinitives: *like, want, need*	• Reflect on the unit question • Connect ideas across readings • Set and achieve goals • Apply unit tips and use *Q Online Practice* to become a strategic learner • Apply information from reading to own situation • Support opinions with reasons	• Describe the duties of the job you want and give reasons that it is a good job for you.
• Match definitions • Define new terms • Understand meaning from context • Learn word roots to expand vocabulary	• *There* and *to be* in the simple present and simple past	• Reflect on the unit question • Connect ideas across readings • Set and achieve goals • Apply unit tips and use *Q Online Practice* to become a strategic learner • Support opinions with examples • Express likes and preferences • Apply information from reading to own situation	• Explain how a place changed because of international immigration or culture.
• Match definitions • Define new terms • Understand meaning from context • Use phrasal verbs to expand vocabulary	• Simple past with regular and irregular verbs	• Reflect on the unit question • Connect ideas across readings • Set and achieve goals • Apply unit tips and use *Q Online Practice* to become a strategic learner • Compare different ways of thinking about a topic • Apply information from reading to own situation	• Write about a time when you or someone you know changed a situation with positive thinking.

UNIT	READING	WRITING
5 Vacation **Why is vacation important?** **READING 1: Vacation from Work** An Email (Vacation) **READING 2: Vacation from School** Letters to the Editor (Opinion)	• Preview text • Read for main ideas • Read for details • Use glosses and footnotes to aid comprehension • Read and recognize different text types • Use photos/pictures to activate schema before reading • Read charts, graphs, and tables to organize and interpret information and statistics • Compare information in readings to see similarities and differences	• Plan before writing • Revise, edit, and rewrite • Write paragraphs of different genres • Give feedback to peers and self-assess • Use topic sentences, supporting sentences, and concluding sentences to write a well formed paragraph • Write a paragraph giving reasons
6 Laughter **What makes you laugh?** **READING 1: What Is Laughter?** A News Magazine Article (Laughter) **READING 2: The Best Medicine Is Laughter** A Website Article (Health)	• Preview text • Read for main ideas • Read for details • Use glosses and footnotes to aid comprehension • Read and recognize different text types • Use photos/pictures to activate schema before reading • Identify topic sentences to aid comprehension of text	• Plan before writing • Revise, edit, and rewrite • Write paragraphs of different genres • Give feedback to peers and self-assess • Construct a good topic sentence to make ideas clear when writing • Write a paragraph of explanation
7 Music **How does music make you feel?** **READING 1: Music and Shopping** A Textbook Excerpt (Marketing) **READING 2: Music and the Movies** A Website Article (The Arts)	• Preview text • Read for main ideas • Read for details • Use glosses and footnotes to aid comprehension • Read and recognize different text types • Use photos/pictures to activate schema before reading • Identify supporting sentences and details to aid comprehension of text	• Plan before writing • Revise, edit, and rewrite • Write paragraphs of different genres • Give feedback to peers and self-assess • Write supporting sentences and details to support topic sentences • Write a paragraph about feelings

VOCABULARY	GRAMMAR	CRITICAL THINKING	UNIT OUTCOME
• Match definitions • Define new terms • Understand meaning from context • Identify compound nouns to expand vocabulary	• Conjunction: *because*	• Reflect on the unit question • Connect ideas across readings • Set and achieve goals • Apply unit tips and use *Q Online Practice* to become a strategic learner • Apply information from reading to own situation • Identify reasons for/ against a position • Use a chart to organize information	• Write a paragraph explaining how much vacation time you need.
• Match definitions • Define new terms • Understand meaning from context • Use the dictionary to learn parts of speech	• Sentences with *when*	• Reflect on the unit question • Connect ideas across readings • Set and achieve goals • Apply unit tips and use *Q Online Practice* to become a strategic learner • Apply information from reading to own situation • Identify reasons for/ against a position	• Explain what makes you or someone you know laugh.
• Match definitions • Define new terms • Understand meaning from context • Build vocabulary using prefixes: *un-*	• Prepositions of location	• Reflect on the unit question • Connect ideas across readings • Set and achieve goals • Apply unit tips and use *Q Online Practice* to become a strategic learner • Express likes and preferences • Apply ideas from reading to different situations	• Identify what type of music you like, where you listen to it, and how it makes you feel.

UNIT	READING	WRITING
8 Honesty **Is it ever OK to lie?** **READING 1: The Lies People Tell** A Magazine Article (Honesty) **READING 2: Honesty and Parenting** Internet Chat Room Postings (Parenting)	• Preview text • Read for main ideas • Read for details • Use glosses and footnotes to aid comprehension • Read and recognize different text types • Match pronouns with their referents to see text cohesion • Make inferences to deepen comprehension of text • Skim text before reading to get the main idea	• Plan before writing • Revise, edit, and rewrite • Write paragraphs of different genres • Give feedback to peers and self-assess • Write concluding sentences to close a paragraph • Write an opinion paragraph
9 Life Changes **How are children and adults different?** **READING 1: What Is An Adult?** An Excerpt from a Textbook (Life Changes) **READING 2: Becoming an Adult** Magazine Blog Postings (Anthropology)	• Preview text • Read for main ideas • Read for details • Use glosses and footnotes to aid comprehension • Read and recognize different text types • Mark the margins to engage actively with the text • Skim text before reading to get the main idea • Use charts to organize information from reading	• Plan before writing • Revise, edit, and rewrite • Write paragraphs of different genres • Give feedback to peers and self-assess • Construct a timeline to sequence events in a story • Write a narrative paragraph
10 Fear **What are you afraid of?** **READING 1: A Dangerous World?** A Magazine Article (Fear) **READING 2: Can We Trust Our Fears?** An Online Article (Psychology)	• Preview text • Read for main ideas • Read for details • Use glosses and footnotes to aid comprehension • Read and recognize different text types • Use photos/pictures to activate schema before reading • Distinguish fact from opinion to read critically • Scan text to locate facts and opinions	• Plan before writing • Revise, edit, and rewrite • Write paragraphs of different genres • Give feedback to peers and self-assess • Use the transitional expression *however* to contrast ideas in writing • Use correct punctuation with *however* • Write a paragraph of explanation

VOCABULARY	GRAMMAR	CRITICAL THINKING	UNIT OUTCOME
• Match definitions • Define new terms • Understand meaning from context • Learn collocations to expand vocabulary	• Infinitives of purpose: *in order* + infinitive	• Reflect on the unit question • Connect ideas across readings • Set and achieve goals • Apply unit tips and use *Q Online Practice* to become a strategic learner • Express opinions • agreement/disagreement • Use a T-chart to organize information	• Write a paragraph that explains your opinion about whether or not it is OK to lie in an online forum.
• Match definitions • Define new terms • Understand meaning from context • Use the dictionary to identify different definitions of the same word	• Clauses with *after* and *after that*	• Reflect on the unit question • Connect ideas across readings • Set and achieve goals • Apply unit tips and use *Q Online Practice* to become a strategic learner • Apply information from reading to own situation • Identify reasons for/against a position	• Describe events in your life that made you feel like an adult.
• Match definitions • Define new terms • Understand meaning from context • Recognize word families to expand vocabulary	• Comparative adjectives	• Reflect on the unit question • Connect ideas across readings • Set and achieve goals • Apply unit tips and use *Q Online Practice* to become a strategic learner • Justify opinions with reasons	• Describe an unreasonable fear and explain how it can be avoided.

UNIT 1

Names

READING ● scanning for information
VOCABULARY ● using the dictionary
WRITING ● capitalizing proper nouns
GRAMMAR ● simple present

LEARNING OUTCOME

Write about a name that you like, giving information about the name.

Unit QUESTION

How did you get your name?

PREVIEW THE UNIT

A Discuss these questions with your classmates.

What boys' names do you like?

What girls' names do you like?

Look at the photo. Which name is the most interesting to you? Why?

B Discuss the Unit Question above with your classmates.

Listen to *The Q Classroom*, Track 2 on CD 1, to hear other answers.

C **Work with a partner. Look at the student's ID card. Then answer the questions.**

	Me	My partner
1. What is your full name?	___	___
2. What is your family name?	___	___
3. What is your given name?	___	___
4. Do you have a middle name? If yes, what is it?	___	___

Tip for Success

In English-speaking countries, the given name is often called the *first name*. The family name is often called the *last name*.

D **Introduce your partner to the class. Tell the class your partner's name.**

READING 1 | Naming Around the World

VOCABULARY

Here are some words from Reading 1. Read the sentences. Then write each bold word next to the correct definition.

1. Let's **choose** a name for our new baby girl. Do you like Amy or Sandra?
2. In China, it is an old **tradition** not to name a child before it is born.
3. Many families have three living **generations**. There are grandparents, parents, and children.
4. He is writing a **poem** about the beauty and joy of having children.
5. Many of my **relatives** have the same name. My grandmother, aunt, and cousin are all named Natalie.
6. Some families make a new name that no one else has. They **create** a name for their child.
7. Many girls in the United States have the name Emma. It is a **popular** name.
8. That name has a nice **sound**. It's nice to say and to hear.

a. ________________ (*noun*) people in your family

b. ________________ (*noun*) all the people in a family of about the same age

c. ________________ (*verb*) to decide which thing or person you want

d. ________________ (*noun*) something you hear

e. ________________ (*noun*) the way people do something for many years

f. ________________ (*adjective*) liked by a lot of people

g. ________________ (*noun*) words written in short lines to show ideas and feelings

h. ________________ (*verb*) to make something new

PREVIEW READING 1

This is a magazine article about different ways people in the world name children.

Look quickly at the article. Which three groups of people is the article about? Write them below.

1. ______________________ 3. ______________________

2. ______________________

CD 1 Track 3 **Read the article.**

Naming Around the World

1 There are many ways to **choose** a name for a child. The following are **traditions** from three groups of people.

Chinese Naming Tradition

2 Many Chinese names have three parts: the family name (or last name), the **generation** name, and the given name (or first name).

3 The last name comes from the father's family. There are not many different last names in China. More than half of all Chinese people have one of these last names: Chen, Lin, Huang, Lee, Zhang, Wu, Wang, Cai, or Liu.

4 The generation name comes from the words in a **poem**. Traditionally, each family has its own "generation poem." The first generation uses the first word in the poem for its generation name. The second generation uses the second word, and so on.

5 The first name can be almost any word in Chinese. Often girls' names are words for beauty or flowers and boys' names are words for strength and health. Usually the Chinese don't name their children after famous people or **relatives**.

African-American Naming Tradition

6 Today in the United States, many African Americans have European last names. Some choose European first names for their children, but many do not. Some choose African names. Some choose Arabic names. Some **create** a whole new name for their child.

Members of the Wong Family

Family Member	Family (Last) Name	Generation Name	Given (First) Name
Father / husband	Wong	Shen	Jian
Mother / wife	Chen	Han	Song
Son 1	Wong	Qi	Li
Son 2	Wong	Qi	Bei
Daughter 1	Wong	Qi	Jun
Mother's sister / aunt	Chen	Han	Tang

7 Parents first choose a **popular** name, and then they change it a little to make it interesting. For example, they start with the name *Mark* and then add *quon* to create the new name *Marquon*. Other parents create a name that has a nice **sound**. Parents choose different sounds to create a new, interesting name. The chart shows popular sounds and examples of names for boys and girls.

famous basketball player LeBron James

Popular Sounds in African-American Names

Beginning Sounds	End Sounds	Names
Chan- De- Ja- Ka- La-	For Girls -isha -ique -ika -ella	For Girls Katisha Shanique Wanika Chantella
Le- Ni- Shan- Tri- Wa-	For Boys -el -on -onte -quon	For Boys Denzel Lebron Kavonte Dequon

Spanish Naming Tradition

8 In Spain, a name usually has three parts: the first name, the father's last name, and the mother's last name. The father's last name is used from one generation to the next. The mother's last name goes only to one generation—to her sons and daughters.

9 Traditionally, parents give their children the grandparents' first names. They name the first boy after the father's father. They name the first girl after the father's mother. Parents name the second boy after the mother's father and the second girl after the mother's mother. The child's name tells the family history.

Main Ideas

Read the statements. Write *T* (true) or *F* (false).

F 1. People all over the world name children the same way.

___ 2. People in the same family usually share the same last name.

___ 3. A person's name can tell a story about that person's family.

___ 4. Most naming traditions are the same.

Details

Tip Critical Thinking

The Details activity asks you to **identify** the tradition. Identifying information is one way to show you have learned the material.

Read the statements. For each statement, check (✓) the tradition(s) the reading talks about.

	Chinese	African American	Spanish
1. The sound of the name is important.		✓	
2. The first name means something in the language.			
3. The first name is from a relative.			
4. Family members in the same generation share a name.			
5. The last name is from the father.			
6. The last names are from the mother and father.			
7. The parents create a name for the child.			

Reading Skill Scanning for information

Scanning is reading very quickly to find pieces of information in a text. For example, you scan a phone book for a name or number. You move your eyes quickly over the text. You do not read every word. You look for the words or information you want.

Scanning can help you answer questions quickly. Follow these steps.

1. Read the question. Underline the important word or words in the question.
2. Scan the reading text for the words you underlined.
3. Circle the information you need in the reading text.
4. Write the answer to the question.

A. **Scan Reading 1 to answer each question. Scan for the underlined words in the questions and circle the information in the text. Then write your answer.**

1. What are the three parts of a Spanish name?

   (1) ______the given name______

   (2) ____________________

   (3) ____________________

2. What is an example of an African-American boy's name? ____________

B. **Scan Reading 1 again to answer the questions. Remember to underline the important words in the questions and to scan for them in the text.**

1. What are two Chinese relatives with the same generation name?

   ____________________ ____________________

2. What are two examples of African-American girls' names?

   ____________________ ____________________

3. What are two examples of Spanish family names?

   ____________________ ____________________

WHAT DO YOU THINK?

Complete the activities.

1. Read each statement. Is it true for your family? Check (✓) *Yes* or *No*.

	Yes	No
1. We give our children the names of people in our family.	☐	☐
2. We give each child a unique name.	☐	☐
3. We give our children the mother's family name.	☐	☐
4. We give our children the father's family name.	☐	☐
5. We make new names.	☐	☐
6. We choose names in a different way.	☐	☐

2. Work with a partner. Discuss your answers in Activity 1. Give examples from your family for your *Yes* answers. Then for one example write 2 to 3 sentences in your notebook.

We give our children the names of people in our family. My father's name is Dan. My brother's name is Dan, too.

READING 2 | Naming the BlackBerry

VOCABULARY

Here are some words from Reading 2. Read the sentences. Then write each bold word next to the correct definition.

1. Almost 5,000 people work for that car **company**. It makes great cars.
2. The new cleaning **product** is good. Everybody is buying it.
3. Please **describe** your brother to me. Is he tall? What color is his hair?
4. People use **electronics** every day. Cell phones and computers are everywhere.
5. Two highways and a train line **connect** New York with Boston.
6. The names Alexander and Alexandra are **similar**, but one is a boy's name, and the other is a girl's name.
7. An interesting name gets people's **attention**. They look at it and think about it.

a. ___electronics___ (*noun*) things like computers and televisions

b. ________________ (*verb*) to join one thing to another thing

c. ________________ (*adjective*) the same in some ways but not completely the same

d. ________________ (*noun*) the state of looking or listening carefully and with interest

e. ________________ (*verb*) to say what someone or something is like

f. ________________ (*noun*) a group of people who work together to make or sell things

g. ________________ (*noun*) something that people make or grow to sell

PREVIEW READING 2

This is an online article about how a product got its name.

Look at the title and photos. Check (✓) the answer you think is true.

What product is the article about?

☐ a type of phone ☐ a type of fruit

Read the article.

Naming the BlackBerry®

1 The **company** Lexicon Branding helps companies find good names for their **products**. A good name is easy to say. A good name **describes** a product well. And a good name gives people a new way of thinking about a product.

2 The Canadian company RIM makes **electronics**. In 2000, RIM had a new product. It was a small phone with e-mail and Internet. They named it *PocketLink*. This name described the product. The product was easy to carry in a pocket, and it **connected**, or linked[1], to other phones and to the Internet. But RIM didn't like the name *PocketLink*. They wanted something interesting. They wanted something unique.

3 Lexicon thought[2] of a new name. The name was *Blackberry*. A blackberry is a small, black fruit. The blackberry fruit connects to other blackberries on vines[3]. The BlackBerry® looks **similar** to a blackberry. It is small and black. A BlackBerry® connects to other BlackBerry® electronics on the Internet. The name *BlackBerry* describes the product well.

4 People think of good things when they think about blackberries. Blackberries are easy to pick[4]. They are fun to eat. The fruit is delicious. People don't usually think

Blackberries on a vine

[1] **link:** to join one person or thing to another
[2] **thought:** past form of the verb *to think*
[3] **vine:** a long, climbing plant
[4] **pick:** to take a flower, fruit, or vegetable from the place where it grows

small electronics are fun and easy. The name *BlackBerry* changes the way people think about the product. Lexicon Branding's website says, "A good name gets your **attention**. A great name changes your thinking."

5 The word *blackberry* also has a nice sound and look. The letter *b* is easy to say. People like to say words that *repeat* sounds. The two *b*s in *black* and *berry* have a nice sound. The name *BlackBerry* also looks good with two capital *B*s.

6 Here is another reason the name *BlackBerry* is a good name. It is unique. No other product has the name. With so many new electronics, it is difficult to get attention. The name *BlackBerry* gets a lot of attention, thanks to Lexicon Branding.

A BlackBerry®

Main Ideas

Read the statements. Write *T* (true) or *F* (false).

Tip for Success

Read a text two times or more. The first time, read quickly for the main ideas. Then read it again for the details.

____ **1.** Blackberries grow on the Internet.

____ **2.** A good product name can help a company.

____ **3.** Fruit and electronics are similar.

____ **4.** The name *BlackBerry* is popular.

Details

Why is *BlackBerry* a good name? Scan Reading 2. Then check (✓) the reasons.

____ **1.** It describes the product well.

____ **2.** It is popular with young people.

____ **3.** It changes your thinking.

____ **4.** It is similar to the names of other electronics.

____ **5.** It has a nice sound.

___ 6. It looks good.

___ 7. It is easy to say.

___ 8. It is an old name.

WHAT DO YOU THINK?

A. Complete the tasks in a group.

1. Think of the names of products you know. Write them in the chart.

Names of Products		
Clothes	Cars	Electronics

Tip for Success

The word *sound* is both a noun and a verb.

2. Discuss the product names. Use these ideas from Reading 2 or your own ideas.

describes the product well	gets your attention	has a nice sound
is easy to say	looks good	

3. Complete the sentences. Write the reasons you talked about in Activity 2.

   a. I like the name ______________________.

   Reason: ______________________________________

   b. I don't like the name ______________________.

   Reason: ______________________________________

B. Think about both Reading 1 and Reading 2 as you discuss the questions.

1. What first names are popular for people in your grandparents' generation?
2. Do people's names change the way we think about them?

Vocabulary Skill | Using the dictionary

A dictionary is a good way to learn new words, and learn how to use them. To find words in a dictionary, you need to know their order. Words in the dictionary are in alphabetical order. In other words, they follow the order of the alphabet (*a*, *b*, *c*). Here are tips to help you find words in a dictionary.

- When the first letter of each word is the same, the second letter is in order.

  ball
  bicycle
  boat

- When the second letter of each word is also the same, the third letter is in order.

  more
  most
  mother

- Short words come before long words when the beginning letters are the same.

child	**tradition**	**popular**
children	**traditional**	**popularity**

A. Find each word in your dictionary. Write the word before it and the word after it.

1. ________________
   attention
   ____

2. ________________
   electronics
   ____

3. ________________
   popular
   ____

4. ________________
   similar
   ____

B. **Write each group of words in alphabetical order.**

1. tradition ______________________

   parent ______________________

   world ______________________

   baby ______________________

2. number ______________________

   name ______________________

   next ______________________

   not ______________________

3. family ______________________

   father ______________________

   famous ______________________

   fast ______________________

4. any ______________________

   after ______________________

   also ______________________

   and ______________________

5. choose ______________________

   child ______________________

   can ______________________

   children ______________________

6. there ______________________

   the ______________________

   then ______________________

   their ______________________

WRITING

Writing Skill | Capitalizing proper nouns

A **noun** is a person, place, or thing. Nouns can be **proper nouns** or **common nouns**.

A proper noun is the name of a person, place, or thing. Proper nouns are always capitalized. This means some or all of the words begin with capital letters.

A common noun is a word for any person, place, or thing. Common nouns are usually only capitalized at the beginning of a sentence.

Proper Nouns	Common Nouns
Maria Perez	woman
Tokyo	city
New Zealand	country
Spanish	nationality

Note: Many proper nouns have more than one word. Small words such as *the* and *of* are not usually capitalized in proper nouns.

the English Channel the Gulf of Mexico

A. Read the sentences. Then find the seven proper nouns and underline them. Remember that many proper nouns have more than one word.

Chicago

I like the name of my city, Chicago. The city is in the state of Illinois in the United States of America. The name comes from the Native Americans. The Algonquins lived on the Chicago River. The word *chigagou* comes from their language. It means *field of onions*. A long time ago, onions grew next to the river and Lake Michigan. I like the name because it is interesting. There is no other place in the world with the same name.

B. **Read each pair of nouns. Which is the common noun? Which is the proper noun? Write each proper noun with a capital letter.**

1. boy	william	William
2. broadway	street	________
3. computer	toshiba	________
4. subaru	car company	________
5. friday	day of the week	________
6. hard rock cafe	restaurant	________
7. november	month	________
8. paris	place	________
9. teacher	ms. andrews	________
10. mountain	mount everest	________

C. **Capitalize the proper nouns in the paragraph.**

I like the name ^C^celedonio. It is a name for a man. It comes from two different languages—spanish and latin. It means *gift from the sky.* It is an unusual name. Not many people have it. The only well-known person with this name was celedonio romero. He was a guitar player from the city of malaga in spain. I like the name because it is an old family name. It is my grandfather's name and my brother's name.

Grammar Simple present 

There are three main ways to use the **simple present**.

- Use the simple present to talk about facts, definitions, or general truths.

  Linda **means** pretty in Spanish. Her name **is** nice.

- Use the simple present to describe habits or routines, or things that happen again and again.

  They **don't drive** to work. They **take** the bus.

- Use the simple present to describe states and feelings (with verbs such as *be*, *have*, and *like*).

  She **has** a BlackBerry®. She **likes** electronics.

Simple present statements

Affirmative		Negative	
I You	**like** blackberries.	I You	**do not like** apples.
He She It	**gets** some attention.	He She It	**does not get** a lot of attention.
We You They	**live** in a big city.	We You They	**do not live** in a small town.

Simple present statements with *be*

Affirmative		Negative	
I	**am** tall.	I	**am not** short.
You	**are** a grandfather.	You	**are not** young.
He She It	**is** at work.	He She It	**is not** at home.
We You They	**are** sisters.	We You They	**are not** cousins.

Simple present statements with *have*

Affirmative		Negative	
I You	**have** a nice name.	I You	**do not have** a generation name.
He She It	**has** a good product.	He She It	**does not have** a big company.
We You They	**have** the same last name.	We You They	**do not have** the same first names.

Note: Contractions (short forms) with *be* and *do* are common in informal written language and in spoken language.

Affirmative			Negative		
I am	=	I'm	I am not	=	I'm not
is	=	's	is not	=	isn't or 's not
are	=	're	are not	=	aren't or 're not
			do not	=	don't
			does not	=	doesn't

A. Circle the correct verb.

1. Some Arab names (is / are) long.
2. They (has / have) four parts.
3. The parents (give / gives) the child a personal name.
4. The child also (gets / get) the father's and the grandfather's given name.
5. The family (gives / give) the child the family name.
6. The names (means / mean) something in their language.
7. *Karim* (mean / means) generous.

B. **Complete each sentence with the correct form of the verb in parentheses.**

Tip for Success

Make sure the simple present verb is correct when the subject is *he*, *she*, or *it*.

1. Names ___*are*___ (be) very important in every country.
2. In India, people ____________ (have) an interesting way to name children.
3. The family ____________ (not, name) the baby for at least ten days.
4. People in the family ____________ (cook) good food for the naming day.
5. Then, the family ____________ (have) a party.
6. A man ____________ (say) important words over the baby.
7. The father ____________ (tell) the child the name in the child's ear.
8. Everyone ____________ (give) food to the child.

Unit Assignment | Write sentences about a name you like

In this assignment, you are going to write sentences about a name you like. Where does it come from? Why do you like it? As you prepare to write, think about the Unit Question, "How did you get your name?" and refer to the Self-Assessment checklist on page 22.

For alternative unit assignments, see the *Q: Skills for Success Teacher's Handbook*.

PLAN AND WRITE

A. **BRAINSTORM** **Work with a partner. Think of names for the topics in the chart. Write three names for each topic.**

Names for People	Names for Products	Names for Places
Emma	Mustang (car)	Dallas, Texas

B. PLAN Discuss these questions with your partner.

1. Choose one of the names that you like from Activity A. Is it a name for a person, product, or place?
2. What do you know about the name?
   - Is it an old name or a new name?
   - Where is the name from?
   - Does the name have a special meaning?
3. Why is it a good name?
   - Is it interesting?
   - Do you like the look of the name?
   - Do you like the sound of the name?
   - Do you like the meaning?

C. WRITE Write four to six sentences about the name in your notebook. Explain why you like the name. Include vocabulary words from this unit and the simple present when you can. Use the information in Activity B to help you. Look at the Self-Assessment checklist on page 22 to guide your writing.

MUSTANG

I like the name Mustang. It is the name of a car.

A mustang is a fast horse.

It is a good name because it is short.

It is easy to say. It gets my attention.

The name Mustang makes me think of going fast.

Revise and Edit

A. **PEER REVIEW** **Work with a partner. Take turns reading your sentences aloud. Then ask your partner these questions.**

1. What is a name I like?
2. Why is it a good name?
3. Are the sentences clear and easy to understand?
4. Do you have any other questions for me?

B. **REWRITE** **Review the answers to the questions in Activity A. You may want to revise and rewrite your sentences.**

C. **EDIT** **Complete the Self-Assessment checklist as you prepare to write the final draft of your sentences. Be prepared to hand in your work or discuss it in class.**

SELF-ASSESSMENT		
Yes	No	
☐	☐	Does every sentence have final punctuation? (period, question mark)
☐	☐	Does every sentence have a subject and a verb?
☐	☐	Does every subject and verb agree?
☐	☐	Is the spelling correct? Check a dictionary if you are not sure.
☐	☐	Do the sentences have vocabulary words from the unit?
☐	☐	Are the proper nouns capitalized?
☐	☐	Is the use of the simple present correct?

Track Your Success

Circle the words you learned in this unit.

Nouns	Verbs	Adjectives
attention 🔑	choose 🔑	popular 🔑
company 🔑	connect 🔑	similar 🔑 AWL
electronics	create 🔑 AWL	
generation AWL	describe 🔑	
poem 🔑		
product 🔑		
relative		
sound 🔑		
tradition 🔑 AWL		

🔑 Oxford 2000 keywords

AWL Academic Word List

For more information on the Oxford 2000 keywords and the AWL, see page xi.

Check (✓) the skills you learned. If you need more work on a skill, refer to the page(s) in parentheses.

READING	○	I can scan for information. (p. 8)
VOCABULARY	○	I can use alphabetical order in the dictionary. (p. 14)
WRITING	○	I can capitalize proper nouns. (p. 16)
GRAMMAR	○	I can recognize and use the simple present. (pp. 18–19)
LEARNING OUTCOME	○	I can write about a name that I like, giving information about the name.

UNIT 2

Work

READING ● previewing a text
VOCABULARY ● word forms
WRITING ● writing complete sentences
GRAMMAR ● verbs + infinitives (*like*, *want*, and *need*)

LEARNING OUTCOME

Describe the duties of the job you want and give reasons that it is a good job for you.

Unit QUESTION

What is a good job?

PREVIEW THE UNIT

A Discuss these questions with your classmates.

Do you like to work?

Do you have a job now? Do you want one?

Look at the photo. The people are working in a kitchen. Do their jobs look like good jobs to you?

B Discuss the Unit Question above with your classmates.

Listen to *The Q Classroom*, Track 5 on CD 1, to hear other answers.

C **Work with a partner. Match each job with a picture.**

chef	nurse	salesclerk
construction worker	office worker	truck driver

1. 

2. 

3. 

4. ____________________

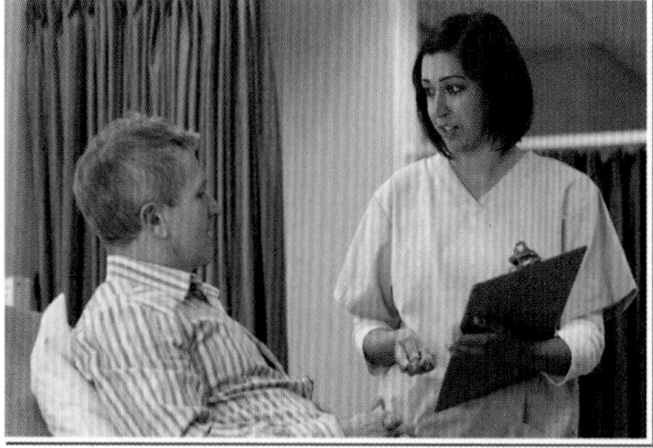

5. ____________________

6. ____________________

D **Ask your partner these questions about each job above.**

1. Does someone you know have this job?
2. Is it a good job? Why or why not?

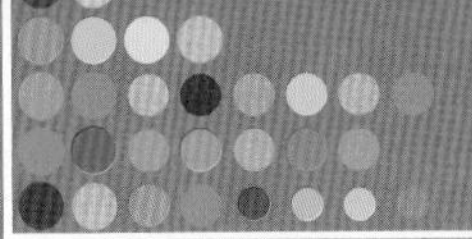

READING

READING 1 | The Right Job for You

VOCABULARY

Here are some words from Reading 1. Read the sentences. Then write each bold word next to the correct definition.

1. She had a 30-year **career** as a nurse at City Hospital.
2. We always **plan** our August vacation in June. We decide where to go.
3. I wish you **success** in your new job.
4. Good nurses have the **skill** to help people who are sick.
5. I like working **outside**. I don't like working in a building.
6. It is a difficult problem. I cannot **solve** it.
7. They think of great names for products. They are very **creative**.
8. I have a difficult **decision**. Do I get a job or go to college?

a. ________________ (*verb*) to decide what you are going to do and how

b. ________________ (*noun*) a choice made after thinking

c. ________________ (*noun*) a job that you learn to do and then do for many years

d. ________________ (*adverb*) not inside a building

e. ________________ (*noun*) the act of doing very well

f. ________________ (*verb*) to find the answer to a question or a problem

g. ________________ (*noun*) a thing you can do well

h. ________________ (*adjective*) having a lot of new ideas or good at making things

Reading Skill | Previewing a text

Good readers **preview** a text (for example, an article, a Web page, or a story) before reading it. They look quickly at the text and its different parts. This helps them understand it. Here are some tips to help you preview.

- Read the **title**. The title is the name of the text.
- Read the **headings**. A heading is a short line of text (like the title). It tells what a section is about. Often there is a heading above each section.
- Look at any pictures and their **captions**. A caption is the text under the picture.

PREVIEW READING 1

This is a Web page for people who are looking for work. Preview the Web page. Then complete the sentences.

1. This is the Web page of a ______.
   a. university b. career center c. newspaper

2. The young person wants to find ______.
   a. a job b. a school c. an office

3. The Web page has ______ steps.
   a. two b. three c. four

CD 1 Track 6 **Read the Web page.**

Winter Hill Career Center

The Right Job for You

What kind of work do you want? What are your skills? What are your interests?

The Winter Hill **Career** Center can help you choose a career!

After you take the test, meet with us. We can help you find work that matches your skills and interests.

Step 1: Take the career test

Step 2: Choose possible careers

Step 3: Visit us and **plan** your career

Step 1: Take the career test

This is the Winter Hill Career Center test. It matches you with possible careers. It Is important that your skills and interests match your career. Happy workers have more **success**. Check (✓) your **skills** and interests to find your worker type[1].

Type 1	☐ I like to be **outside**. ☐ I am good with my hands. ☐ I fix things around the house.	Type 4	☐ I like to talk to different people. ☐ I often plan activities. ☐ I like to help people.
Type 2	☐ I like to **solve** problems. ☐ I like to learn new information. ☐ I like science.	Type 5	☐ I like to talk. ☐ People usually listen to me. ☐ I make **decisions** easily.
Type 3	☐ I like art and music. ☐ I often talk about feelings. ☐ I am **creative**.	Type 6	☐ I follow directions carefully. ☐ I am good with details. ☐ I am good with numbers.

Step 2: Choose possible careers

Which type of worker are you? Look at the boxes with checks (✓). Any section with two or three check marks is your type. Look below for some possible careers for your worker type. Do any of the careers look good to you? We can help you decide.

Type 1: **carpenter, construction worker**

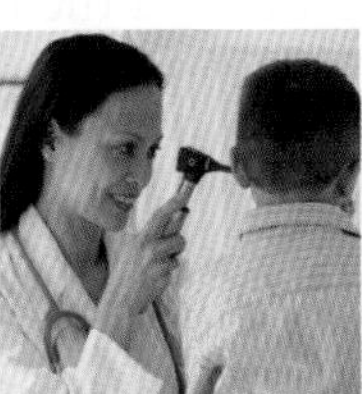

Type 2: **doctor, nurse**

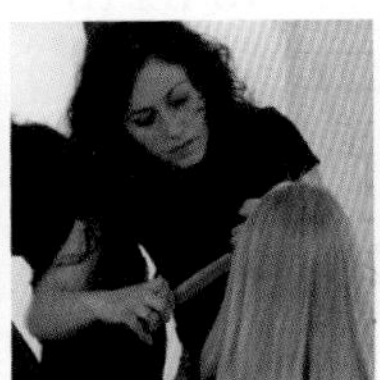

Type 3: **hairdresser, chef**

Type 4: **teacher, tour guide**

Type 5: **lawyer, business person**

Type 6: **accountant, salesclerk**

Step 3: Visit us to plan your career

[1] **worker type:** a group of interests or skills that make a person good for a certain career or job

MAIN IDEAS

Why do people visit the Winter Hill Career Center? Circle two reasons.

a. They are not happy with their jobs.
b. They are happy with their jobs.
c. They want to be students.
d. They want to learn about different jobs and careers.

DETAILS

Tip for Success

To help you answer a question by scanning, remember to underline important words in the question. Scanning for those words makes it easy to find the information.

Which career matches each person's skills and interests? Scan the career test and the possible careers in Reading 1. Then circle the correct answer.

1. I like to help people. I often plan activities.
   a. teacher b. carpenter
2. I like to talk. I make decisions easily.
   a. accountant b. lawyer
3. I'm creative. I like art and music.
   a. hairdresser b. doctor
4. I'm good with numbers. I follow directions carefully.
   a. accountant b. teacher
5. I like science. I like to solve problems.
   a. doctor b. construction worker
6. I'm good with my hands. I like to fix things around the house.
   a. chef b. carpenter

WHAT DO YOU THINK?

Take the career test on page 29. Then discuss the questions in Step 2 in a group.

READING 2 | The World of Work

VOCABULARY

Here are some words from Reading 2. Read their definitions. Then complete each sentence.

duty (*noun*) something you must do because it is part of your job or because you think it is right

flexible (*adjective*) able to change easily

pay (*verb*) to give someone money for something, for example, for work that they do

regular (*adjective*) happening again and again with the same amount of space or time in between

result (*noun*) something that happens because of something else

tour (*noun*) a short visit to see something interesting, like a building or city

1. Her success is the ________________ of many years of hard work.
2. I plan to take a bus ________________ of New York City. It is a very interesting place to visit.
3. My hours are ________________. I always work from 8:00 to 4:00 from Sunday to Thursday.
4. They always ________________ me on Friday. I get 500 dollars a week.
5. One job ________________ of a teacher is correcting homework.
6. This job is different every day. The work always changes. That's why we need ________________ people.

PREVIEW READING 2

Tip for Success

You do not need to understand every word in a reading text. To build your vocabulary, circle the most important four or five new words and find them in the dictionary.

This is a magazine article about different careers.

Preview the article. Look at the questions. What information do you think the people give about their work? Check (✓) your ideas.

☐ 1. the pay
☐ 2. the name of the job
☐ 3. the name of the company
☐ 4. what they do every day at work
☐ 5. what they do at home
☐ 6. what they like about their work

CD 1 Track 7

Read the article.

The World of Work

There are many different kinds of work. People enjoy their work for many different reasons. We talked to four people about their work. Read about their careers.

What do you do? I am a travel agent.

What are your job duties? I plan vacations for people. I buy airplane tickets, get hotel rooms, and plan **tours**.

Why do you like your job? I like helping people solve their travel problems. I work from 9:00 to 5:00 every day. I really like the **regular** hours. And I can buy airplane tickets at very low prices.

What do you do? I am a nurse. I work in a large hospital in the city.

What are your job duties? I help sick people. Day and night, I see that they are OK. I also have to study a lot. I need to know all kinds of information. I follow the doctors' directions very carefully.

Why do you like your job? I know it is important work. I like a quiet workplace. The people are all so nice. I really love my work.

What do you do? I am a salesclerk in an electronics store.

What are your job duties? I need to know all about electronics. I help people make decisions about buying electronics. I tell people about the different products in our store.

Why do you like your job? I like to learn about new electronics. It is always interesting. And they **pay** me very well.

What do you do? I am a Web designer—I make websites. I am self-employed[1]. I work on my computer at home. I make websites for different companies.

What are your job duties? A company asks me to plan a website. I learn about the company and what it needs. I write down some ideas. Then I talk to people at the company again. Then I make the website.

Why do you like your job? I like to be creative. I see the **results** of my work. That makes me happy. Also, I have **flexible** hours. I work at the times I want. I can say no to a job. I work in my home. I have more time with my family.

[1] **self-employed:** working for yourself, not for somebody else

Main Idea

Circle the answer that best completes the statement.

This Web page helps people ______.

a. find a company
b. learn about careers
c. write about their careers

Details

Match the jobs with the job duties.

___ **1.** travel agent	a. telling people about products
___ **2.** nurse	b. creating new pages on the Internet
___ **3.** salesclerk	c. planning vacations for people
___ **4.** Web designer	d. helping sick people

WHAT DO YOU THINK?

A. Discuss the questions in a group.

1. What is important for you in a job? Check (✓) your answers.
   - ☐ nice people
   - ☐ learn about electronics
   - ☐ flexible hours
   - ☐ good pay
   - ☐ regular hours
   - ☐ be creative
   - ☐ a quiet workplace
   - ☐ help solve problems
2. Which career in Reading 2 sounds interesting to you? Why?

B. Think about both Reading 1 and Reading 2 as you discuss the questions.

1. Which job from Reading 1 or Reading 2 do you want to have? Why?

   I want to be a ____________________.

   Reason: ____

   ____

   ____

2. Which job from Reading 1 or Reading 2 do you NOT want to have? Why not?

   I do not want to be a(n) ____________________.

   Reason: ____

   ____

   ____

Vocabulary Skill | Word forms 

Some words are both **nouns** and **verbs.** They look the same, but they work differently in a sentence. A noun refers to a person, place, object, or idea. A verb refers to an action. Learning to use the same word in different forms helps build your vocabulary.

These words from Reading 1 and Reading 2 can be nouns or verbs.

Word	Noun	Verb
match	This job is a **match** for you.	My skills and interests **match** my career.
plan	His **plan** is to go on vacation next month.	I **plan** activities for people in my office.
result	The **result** of his hard work is a good website.	Hard work **results** in success.
tour	I planned a **tour** of Europe.	We **tour** countries by bus.
travel	I enjoy **travel**.	I **travel** a lot for my job.
work	There are many different kinds of **work**.	I **work** in a large hospital in the city.

Tip Critical Thinking

In Activity A, you have to **label** (or name) the word as a noun or a verb. Writing a label on examples of something you have learned is a good way to remember it.

A. Read the paragraph. Write *N* (noun) or *V* (verb) above each bold word.

I am a pilot. I like my **work** (1, N). I need to be very careful. The **result** (2) of bad decisions is sometimes terrible. My job is difficult, but they **pay** (3) me very well. My job is also fun. I **travel** (4) all over Europe. Every time I go to a new city, I take a **tour** (5).

B. Is the bold word a noun or a verb? Check (✓) *Noun* or *Verb*.

	Noun	Verb
1. The **work** of a nurse is taking care of sick people.	☐	☐
2. My father **travels** to many countries for his company.	☐	☐
3. A good career for you **matches** your worker type.	☐	☐
4. A carpenter sees the **results** of his work every day.	☐	☐
5. What is your **plan** for your career?	☐	☐

WRITING

Writing Skill Writing complete sentences

Every **sentence** needs a subject and a verb. The *subject* is who or what the sentence is about. The *verb* tells what the subject does (action) or what the subject thinks, feels, or is (state).

He follows directions very well. (subject: He; verb: follows)

His work is excellent. (subject: His work; verb: is)

Travel agents get low-priced tickets. (subject: Travel agents; verb: get)

They like traveling. (subject: They; verb: like)

A sentence with no subject or no verb is not complete. It is a **sentence fragment**.

✓ **She** likes her new job.
✗ Likes her new job. (no subject)

✓ A carpenter **is** at my house.
✗ A carpenter at my house. (no verb)

Always check your writing and ask, *Does this sentence have a subject? Does this sentence have a verb?* A complete sentence must have a subject and a verb.

A. Read the sentences about truck drivers. Underline the subjects and circle the verbs.

1. A truck driver works in a truck.
2. He drives up to 11 hours a day.
3. Truck drivers travel very far over many days.
4. They sleep in a special bed in the truck.
5. The company pays the driver for the number of miles.
6. A driver needs to arrive on time.

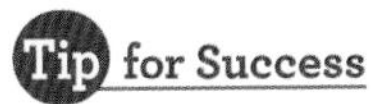

Remember to capitalize the first word in the sentence and put a period at the end.

B. **Choose a subject or verb from the box to make a complete sentence. Then read the information about nurses to a partner.**

~~work~~	wear	help
don't make	the doctor	the nurses

1. nurses / in a hospital

   Nurses work in a hospital.

2. in the hospital, / they / white clothes

   ____

3. they / loud sounds / in the hospital rooms

   ____

4. follow / the doctor's directions

   ____

5. the nurses / the sick people

   ____

6. visits / the sick people / every day

   ____

Grammar Verbs + infinitives (*like*, *want*, and *need*)

Like, *want*, and *need* are common verbs. A noun/noun phrase or an infinitive form of a verb (*to* + base form of the verb) often follows *like*, *want*, or *need*.

Noun phrase	Infinitive
I like **my career**.	I like **to help** people.
I want **a career**.	I want **to be** a doctor.
I need **a good job**.	I need **to work**.

A. **Underline the noun phrases and circle the infinitives after the verbs** ***like, want,*** **and** ***need.***

1. I want to be a chef in a restaurant. I like to work with people. I like good food. I am creative.
2. I want to be an accountant. I like to solve problems in math. I like to work with details. I need good pay.
3. I want to be a truck driver. I like big trucks. I like to work alone. I want to see the country. I need to move around.
4. I want to be an office worker. I like regular hours. I like people. I need a job in an office.

B. **Complete each sentence with your own ideas. Use a noun or a noun phrase and an infinitive with each verb.**

1. I like ________________________________
2. I like ________________________________
3. I don't like ____________________________
4. I don't like ____________________________
5. I want ________________________________
6. I don't want ___________________________
7. I need ________________________________
8. I don't need ___________________________

Unit Assignment | Write sentences about a job that's right for you

In this assignment, you are going to write sentences about a job you want. Describe the job duties. Explain why the job is right for you. As you prepare to write, think about the Unit Question, "What is a good job?" and refer to the Self-Assessment checklist on page 40.

For alternative unit assignments, see the *Q: Skills for Success Teacher's Handbook.*

PLAN AND WRITE

A. BRAINSTORM Complete the activities.

Tip for Success

You can learn about the duties of many jobs on the Internet. Look for *job duties* or *job description*.

1. List three interesting jobs in your notebook. Then write two or three job duties for each.
2. What's important for you in a job? Check (✓) the things that are important. Add two more ideas to the list.

☐ good pay	☐ regular hours
☐ to help people	☐ to see the results of my work
☐ to travel	☐ to work alone
☐ to work with people	☐ to work indoors
☐ to work outside	☐ to work with details
☐ to work with numbers	☐ to work with my hands

☐ ______________________________

☐ ______________________________

B. PLAN Choose a job from your list in Activity A. Answer the questions.

1. What is a good job for you?

   I want to be a(n) ______________________________

2. What are the duties of this job? Write the job and three job duties.

   A(n) ______________ has these duties.

   Duty 1: ______________________________

   Duty 2: ______________________________

   Duty 3: ______________________________

3. Why is it a good job for you? Write three reasons.

   I like ______________________________

   I want ______________________________

   I need ______________________________

C. WRITE Use the information in Activity B to write sentences about a good job for you. Write in your notebook. Look at the Self-Assessment checklist on page 40 to guide your writing.

Revise and Edit

A. PEER REVIEW Read a partner's sentences. Answer the questions and discuss them with your partner.

1. Are there three job duties? Check (✓) each job duty.
2. Are there three reasons it's a good job for your partner? Underline each reason.
3. Is there something you don't understand? Write a question mark (?) next to the sentence.

B. REWRITE Review the answers to the questions in Activity A. You may want to revise and rewrite your sentences.

C. EDIT Complete the Self-Assessment checklist as you prepare to write the final draft of your sentences. Be prepared to hand in your work or discuss it in class.

SELF-ASSESSMENT		
Yes	No	
☐	☐	Does every sentence begin with a capital letter?
☐	☐	Does every sentence have final punctuation? (period, question mark)
☐	☐	Does every sentence have a subject and a verb?
☐	☐	Does every subject and verb agree?
☐	☐	Is the spelling correct? Check a dictionary if you are not sure.
☐	☐	Do the sentences have vocabulary words from the unit?
☐	☐	Are the verbs *like*, *want*, and *need* used correctly?
☐	☐	Are all sentences complete sentences?

Track Your Success

Circle the words you learned in this unit.

Nouns	Verbs	Adjectives
career 🔑	pay 🔑	creative AWL
decision 🔑	plan 🔑	flexible AWL
duty 🔑	solve 🔑	regular 🔑
result 🔑		**Adverb**
skill 🔑		outside 🔑
success 🔑		
tour 🔑		

🔑 Oxford 2000 keywords
AWL Academic Word List

Check (✓) the skills you learned. If you need more work on a skill, refer to the page(s) in parentheses.

READING	○	I can preview a text. (p. 28)
VOCABULARY	○	I can recognize and use words that are both nouns and verbs. (p. 35)
WRITING	○	I can write complete sentences. (p. 36)
GRAMMAR	○	I can recognize and use verbs + infinitives (*like, want,* and *need*). (p. 37)
LEARNING OUTCOME	○	I can describe the duties of the job I want and give reasons that it is a good job for me.

UNIT 3

Long Distance

READING ● skimming for the main idea
VOCABULARY ● word roots
WRITING ● connecting sentences with *and* and *but*
GRAMMAR ● *there is* / *there are* and *there was* / *there were*

LEARNING OUTCOME

Explain how a place changed because of international immigration or culture.

Unit QUESTION

Why do people immigrate to other countries?

PREVIEW THE UNIT

A **Discuss these questions with your classmates.**

Why do people leave their home countries?

Which countries in the world have a lot of immigration?

Look at the photo. Where are these people? What are they doing?

B **Discuss the Unit Question above with your classmates.**

Listen to *The Q Classroom*, Track 8 on CD 1, to hear other answers.

C **Look at the world map with a partner. Say the names of the labeled countries. Draw a line from the name to the country.**

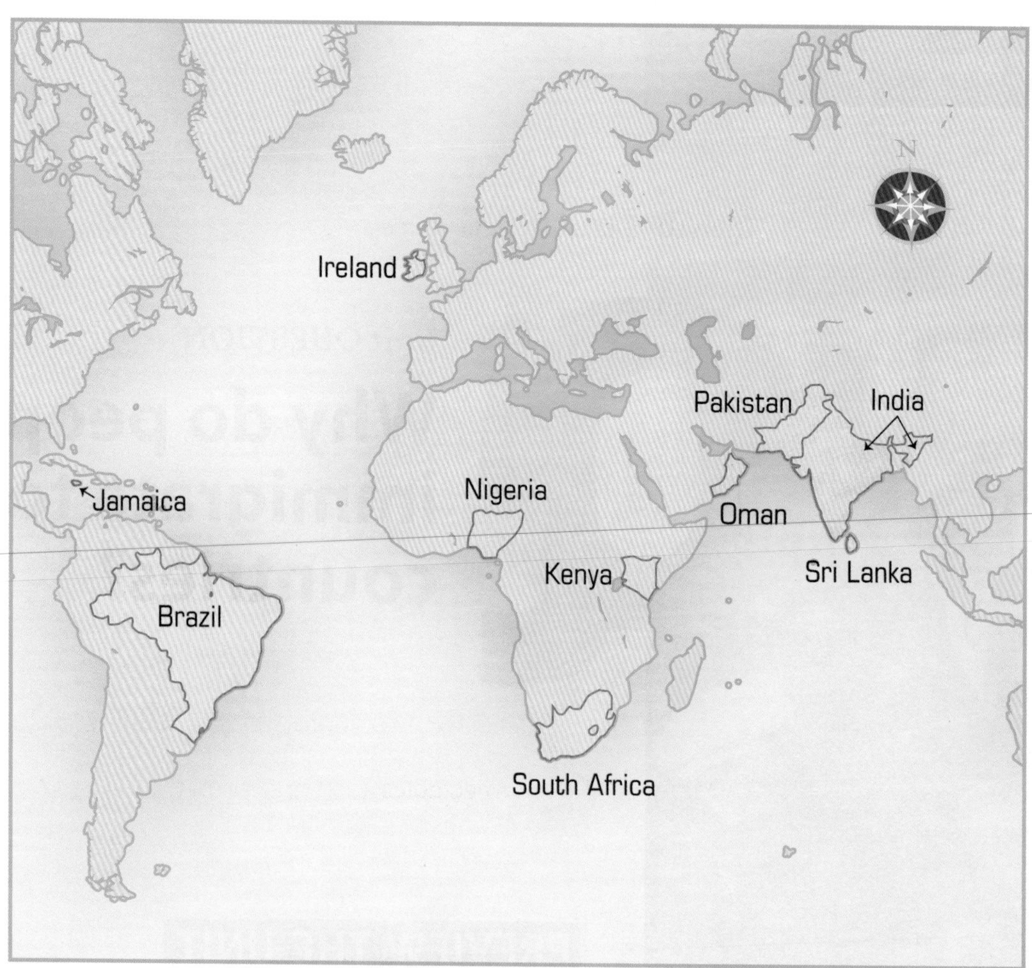

D **Write the names of six other countries you can find on the map. Work with a partner. Point to the countries on the map.**

______________ ______________

______________ ______________

______________ ______________

E **Answer the questions with your partner.**

1. Do you know people from other countries? Which countries?
2. Do you sometimes travel to other countries? Which countries do you visit?

READING

READING 1 | The World in a City

VOCABULARY

Here are some words from Reading 1. Read their definitions. Then complete each sentence.

foreign (*adjective*) belonging to or connected with a country that is not your own
market (*noun*) a place where people go to buy and sell things, usually outside
million (*noun*) 1,000,000
mix (*verb*) to put different things together to make something new
neighborhood (*noun*) a part of a town or city; the people who live there
population (*noun*) the number of people who live in a place
worldwide (*adverb*) existing or happening everywhere in the world

1. In New York City, many people speak English and Spanish. They often ________________ the two languages in a language called *Spanglish.*
2. Many people buy vegetables and fruits at their local ________________.
3. Thanks to the Internet, information travels ________________ in just seconds.
4. Many ________________ students come from Africa and Asia to study in England.
5. Tokyo is a very large city. About 13 ________________ people live there.
6. People in this country don't have many children. The ________________ is going down.
7. I want to live in this ________________. The houses and the gardens are very nice.

PREVIEW READING 1

This is a Web page from a London travel website.

Look at the title, headings, pictures, and captions. What does the website say about London? Check (✓) the answer.

☐ 1. London is fun for families.

☐ 2. There are people from many different countries in London.

☐ 3. People from London like to visit many countries.

CD 1
Track 9

Read the Web page.

The World in a City

London

1 Do you plan to visit London? There are many English sights[1] to see, but there are many other sights, sounds, and foods too. London is a city with many different groups of people with foods, clothes, dances, and many other things from around the world. In a visit to London, you see the world.

Population

2 The **population** of the city of London is about seven **million**. Over two million of these people are from **foreign** countries. People speak over 300 different languages in London.

Eat

3 There is food from more than 55 different countries in London's restaurants. There is even food from countries such as Tanzania, Peru, and Mongolia. At food **markets**, you can buy vegetables and fruits from all over the world.

A festival in London

The following are the top ten countries of origin[2] for today's immigrants in London:

1. India
2. Ireland
3. Bangladesh
4. Jamaica
5. Nigeria
6. Pakistan
7. Kenya
8. Sri Lanka
9. Ghana
10. Cyprus

[1] **sights:** interesting places to see

[2] **country of origin:** the country a person comes from

See

4 In the **neighborhoods** of London, there are people from many countries with many different ways of living. You can go to festivals and see different clothing and dances. You can go to London's many museums and see old and new art from all over the world.

Hear

5 London is a center of world music. There are music stores, dance clubs, and radio stations here. London has music from around the world, and people make new kinds of music here too. *Bhangra* music **mixes** the sounds of Punjabi[3] music with popular European and African music. It is now popular **worldwide**.

London's food markets have fruits and vegetables from all over the world.

[3] **Punjabi:** from the province of Punjab in northern India

Reading Skill Skimming for the main idea

Skimming is reading a text quickly to find the **main idea**, or the basic meaning of a text. People often skim articles online, in newspapers, or in magazines. They look quickly at all sections of an article to get the basic information. Then they decide if they want to take more time to read part or all of the article.

Skimming saves time, and it allows you to get the information you want. Here are some tips to help you skim for the main idea of a text.

- Read the title to determine what the text is about.
- Read the headings of any sections to see the organization of the text.
- Read any charts or photos to see what the author is writing about.
- Quickly read the first and last sentence of each paragraph. Often the main idea of a paragraph is at the beginning or the end.

MAIN IDEAS

Circle the best answer to each question.

1. How many sections are there?
   a. 2
   b. 6
   c. 5

2. Does the heading of each section give you an idea of what the section is about?
   a. yes
   b. no
   c. sometimes

3. What does the photo on page 46 tell you about London?
   a. English people like to dance.
   b. People from other countries live in London.
   c. London is big.

4. Which section of Reading 1 gives the overall main idea of the reading?
   a. Section 1: London
   b. Section 2: Population
   c. Section 4: See

DETAILS

Tip for Success

Read all the answers in a multiple-choice exercise before you choose one answer.

Circle the answer that best completes each statement.

1. About ______ foreign-born people live in London.
   a. seven million
   b. two million
   c. three hundred

2. People in London speak over ______ languages.
   a. 55
   b. 250
   c. 300

3. Most foreign-born people in London come from ______.
   a. India, Ireland, and Bangladesh
   b. Jamaica, Nigeria, and Pakistan
   c. Turkey, Spain, and the United States

4. You can buy ______ in London markets.
   a. food from Tanzania and Peru
   b. vegetables and fruits from different parts of the world
   c. food from 55 different restaurants

5. *Bhangra* music mixes music from ______ with popular European and African music.
   a. China
   b. Mexico
   c. India

What Do You Think?

Discuss the questions in a group.

1. Do you like to eat food from different countries? Which foods do you like to eat?
2. Do you like music or dance from other countries? Which music or dance do you like?
3. Do you want to visit London? Do you want to visit another country? Tell your group where you want to visit and why.

READING 2 | Immigrant Stories

Vocabulary

Here are some words from Reading 2. Read the sentences. Then write each bold word next to the correct definition.

1. I'm very lucky. I have the **opportunity** to go to London this year.
2. John doesn't have any friends. He is **lonely**.
3. I work in a restaurant now, but I want to have my **own** restaurant.

4. Children need their parents to **support** them. They need food, money, love, and many other things.
5. One year is not enough. You need **several** years to make a new life in a new country.
6. Many people from Jamaica live in London. They have a large **community** there.
7. People from many different countries live and work in London. It is an **international** city.

a. ________________ (*noun*) a group of people who are together, for example, because they have the same interests or background

b. ________________ (*verb*) to help someone to live by giving them things like money, a home, or food

c. ________________ (*adjective*) unhappy because you are not with other people

d. ________________ (*adjective*) belonging to a particular person

e. ________________ (*noun*) a chance to do something

f. ________________ (*adjective*) more than two but not many

g. ________________ (*adjective*) between different countries

PREVIEW READING 2

You are going to read a magazine article that tells the stories of three immigrants.

Skim the article. Then write *T* (true) or *F* (false) for each statement.

___ **1.** The three immigrants all tell about living in London.

___ **2.** They all tell about things that happen in their lives.

___ **3.** The three immigrants work together and are friends.

CD 1
Track 10 **Read the magazine article.**

Immigrant Stories

1 **Immigrants in London—Why are they in London? Are they happy to live here? Do they plan to stay? Read their stories and find the answers!**

Story 1: Sun Yun Wing

2 My name is Sun Yun Wing. I am from a small town near Hong Kong. In 1960, there weren't many jobs there. There were many job **opportunities** in England. So, I came to London. I was 20 years old.

Sun Yun Wing with his wife

3 There were many problems at first. The English language was hard for me, and the weather was cold and rainy. I was **lonely** because my family wasn't with me, but there were good things about living in London. There were many jobs with good pay.

4 My first job was in a Chinese restaurant. Now, I have my **own** restaurant. I work there with my wife. She is also Chinese. Her English is good. She talks to the customers. I am the chef. We work very hard.

5 We have three children. They have good jobs. They do not want to go and live in Hong Kong. My wife and I don't know anyone in Hong Kong now. Our life is here. This is our home.

Story 2: Basher Ali

6 My name is Basher Ali. I am from a small town in Bangladesh. I came to England in 1980 with my wife and two small children. I was 25 years old. There were many jobs in England. It was the best way to **support** my family.

7 My first job in England was in a factory[1]. At night, I went to school. There were classes in English and business. I was happy to be a student. There were no opportunities for me to go to school in my hometown in Bangladesh.

8 Now, I have my own business. I sell clothing from Bangladesh. My business is very successful. I have **several** clothing stores.

Basher Ali

[1] **factory:** a place where people make things, usually with machines

9 I try to help my people. In London, I hold English classes at my stores for the Bangladeshi **community**. I send money to my relatives and my town in Bangladesh. I support a children's language school there.

10 I have good children. They work in my company. They keep Bangladeshi ways in their families. They have success in England, but they are still Bangladeshi in their hearts.

Story 3: Apara Asuquo

Apara Asuquo

11 My name is Apara Asuquo. I am from Nigeria. I came to London in 2003 with my husband. I was 45 years old. My husband works for an **international** bank here in London. There was an office of the same bank in Nigeria. We came here for his career.

12 I was a businesswoman[2] in my country. Here, there were no good jobs for me. After two years, my husband said, "This is a different country. This is your new life. You need to start from the beginning again." Now, I am an office worker. The pay isn't very good, but I like the people.

13 Our children go to university in England. My husband and I plan to return to Nigeria, but our children plan to stay here. There are many opportunities for them here. It is always sad to say goodbye, but for my husband and me, Nigeria is our home.

[2] **businesswoman:** a woman who works in business, especially in a top position

MAIN IDEAS

Tip for Success

As you use this book, review the reading skills from earlier lessons. Practice these skills as you read new texts.

Circle the answer to each question.

Sun Yun Wing

1. Is he happy living in England? Yes No
2. Does he plan to stay? Yes No

Basher Ali

3. Is he happy living in England? Yes No
4. Does he plan to stay? Yes No

Apara Asuquo

5. Is she happy living in England? Yes No
6. Does she plan to stay? Yes No

DETAILS

Read the stories again. Check (✓) the problems and successes of each immigrant. You may check (✓) more than one person for each statement.

	Sun Yun Wing	Basher Ali	Apara Asuquo
1. I was lonely.	☐	☐	☐
2. The language was hard.	☐	☐	☐
3. There were no good jobs.	☐	☐	☐
4. I was sad without my family.	☐	☐	☐
5. I have a business in England.	☐	☐	☐
6. I help my community.	☐	☐	☐
7. My children go to university in England.	☐	☐	☐
8. My children have good jobs.	☐	☐	☐

WHAT DO YOU THINK?

A. Discuss the questions in a group. Then choose one question and write 2 to 3 sentences in response.

1. In the Details activity above, numbers 1–4 tell about problems immigrants have in London. What problems do immigrants have in your town, city, or country?
2. In the Details activity, numbers 5–8 tell about successes London immigrants have. What are the successes of immigrants in your town, city, or country?

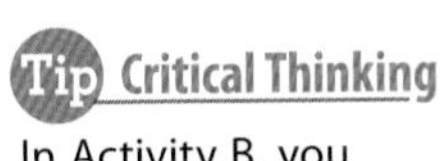

In Activity B, you have to **restate**, or say again in perhaps a different way, some of the information you learned in the two readings. **Restating** is a good way to review information.

B. Think about both Reading 1 and Reading 2 as you discuss the questions.

1. Is immigration good for countries like England?
2. What are the good things for the country?
3. What are the problems?

Vocabulary Skill | Word roots 

The **root** of a word is the part of a word with the basic meaning.

lone	a**lone**
lonely	**lone**liness

The root is *lone*, which means *without another person*. The meaning of each of the words relates to this basic meaning. Learning roots can increase your vocabulary and help you guess the meaning of a new word in a text.

A. **These words from the unit have word roots (in bold). Match each word root with its definition.**

factory	im**migra**te	inter**nat**ional	**pop**ulation

	Word Roots	Definitions
___ 1.	nat	a. people
___ 2.	pop	b. to do or make
___ 3.	fac	c. to be born or come from
___ 4.	migra	d. to move

B. **Here are more words with the same roots. Match each word with its definition.**

	Words	Definitions
___ 1.	migrate	a. belonging to a place from birth
___ 2.	native	b. to fill an area with people
___ 3.	populate	c. to make things using machines
___ 4.	manufacture	d. to leave your country for another country

WRITING

Writing Skill | Connecting sentences with *and* and *but*

You can connect two simple sentences with *and* to give more information. Use a comma before *and*.

I like to eat Indian food, **and** I like to listen to *Bhangra*.
I am 25 years old, **and** I have two small children.

You can connect two simple sentences with *but* to give opposite or different information. Use a comma before *but*.

They are happy, **but** they miss their home.
She likes the English language, **but** she doesn't like English weather.

A. Complete each sentence with *and* or *but*. Remember to use *but* for different information.

1. He works as a chef, ____and____ his brother does too.
2. There are great opportunities for immigrants, ________ there are also many problems for them.
3. I made eggs for breakfast, ________ they didn't taste good.
4. She is from India, ________ she speaks English very well.
5. She was a teacher in her country, ________ she isn't a teacher in the United States.
6. He is in Africa, ________ his family is there too.

B. Read the sentences. Then connect them with *and* or *but*. Use commas.

1. Ana likes England.
   She wants to visit Mexico.

   Ana likes England, but she wants to visit Mexico.

2. There are not many Chinese people here.
   Chang is lonely.

   ____

3. There is a lot of world music in London.
   There is a lot of English music too.

   ____

4. There are not many Mexicans in New York City.
   There are many immigrants from the Dominican Republic.

   ____

5. She really wants to work.
   She doesn't have a job.

   ____

Grammar *There is / there are* and *there was / there were*

When talking about the location of something or someone, you can use *there* + *be*. In most sentences, the verb comes after the noun phrase. With *there* + *be*, *be* comes before the noun phrase.

Simple present

There is a restaurant on Smith Street. (*be* = is; noun phrase = a restaurant)
There are restaurants near the station. (*be* = are; noun phrase = restaurants)

Simple past

There was a music store on the corner. (*be* = was; noun phrase = a music store)
There were music stores on Broadway. (*be* = were; noun phrase = music stores)

One way to make *there* + *be* sentences negative is to add *no*.

There is no movie theater in my town.
There is no grass in the park.
There are no parking lots.
There was no pet store in my old neighborhood.
There were no tall buildings on Broadway back then.

The Statue of Liberty

Circle the correct verb.

1. In 1880, there (was / were) 12,000 Italians in New York City.
2. By 1910, there (was / were) a large Italian population.
3. There (was / were) 341,000 people from Italy in New York City.
4. In New York City today, there (is / are) about three million immigrants.
5. There (is / are) eight million people in New York City.

6. Today, there (is / are) students from 172 different countries in the City University of New York.

7. There (is / are) several reasons people come to New York City.

8. Sometimes, there (is / are) problems in the home country.

9. There (is / are) an opportunity to make good money.

10. There (is / are) good jobs.

11. Also, there (is / are) often a friend who already lives in New York City.

12. There (is / are) always a place to stay.

Unit Assignment | Write sentences about a place that is changing

In this assignment, you are going to write sentences about a place that is changing because of international immigration or international culture. Use information from the reading texts and from your work in the unit to help you. As you prepare to write, think about the Unit Question, "Why do people immigrate to other countries?" and refer to the Self-Assessment checklist on page 58.

For alternative unit assignments, see the *Q: Skills for Success Teacher's Handbook*.

PLAN AND WRITE

web Your Writing Process
For this activity, you could also use Stage 1A, *Freewriting* in *Q Online Practice.*

A. BRAINSTORM Complete the activities.

1. Think about a place that immigration is changing. Write the name of the place.

2. How is immigration or international culture changing this place? Think about the place now and in the past. What are some changes in businesses, restaurants, supermarkets, languages people speak, music, art, schools, and families? Also remember changes you read about in this unit.

B. PLAN Complete the sentences about the place today and in the past. Use vocabulary from the unit.

______________________ Today and in the Past
(name of place)

1. In the past, there (was / were) ______________________, but today there (is / are) ______________________.

2. In the past, there (was / were) ______________________, but today there (is / are) ______________________.

3. Today, there (is / are) ______________________.

4. Today, there (is / are) ______________________.

5. In the past, there (was / were) ______________________.

6. In the past, there (was / were) ______________________.

C. WRITE Write your sentences in your notebook. Look at the Self-Assessment checklist below to guide your writing.

REVISE AND EDIT

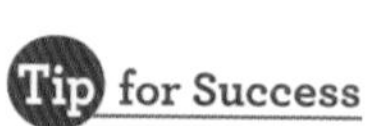

To check your writing, read it aloud to yourself or a partner. When you read aloud, you can find your mistakes more quickly.

A. PEER REVIEW Read a partner's sentences. Answer the questions and discuss them with your partner.

1. Do the sentences discuss what the place was like in the past?
2. Do the sentences discuss what the place is like now?
3. Is there something you don't understand? Write a question mark (?) next to the sentence.

B. REWRITE Review the answers to the questions in Activity A. You may want to revise and rewrite your sentences.

C. EDIT Complete the Self-Assessment checklist as you prepare to write the final draft of your sentences. Be prepared to hand in your work or discuss it in class.

SELF-ASSESSMENT		
Yes	No	
☐	☐	Does every sentence begin with a capital letter?
☐	☐	Does every sentence have final punctuation? (period, question mark)
☐	☐	Does every sentence have a subject and a verb?
☐	☐	Does every subject and verb agree?
☐	☐	Is the spelling correct? Check a dictionary if you are not sure.
☐	☐	Do the sentences have vocabulary words from the unit?
☐	☐	Is the use of *there* + *be* correct in the present and the past?
☐	☐	Are the sentences connected with *and* and *but* correct?

Track Your Success

Circle the words you learned in this unit.

Nouns	**Verbs**	**Adjectives**
community 🔑 AWL	mix 🔑	foreign 🔑
market 🔑	support 🔑	international 🔑
million		lonely 🔑
neighborhood		own 🔑
opportunity 🔑		several 🔑
population		**Adverb**
		worldwide

🔑 Oxford 2000 keywords

AWL Academic Word List

Check (✓) the skills you learned. If you need more work on a skill, refer to the page(s) in parentheses.

READING	I can skim for the main idea. (p. 47)
VOCABULARY	I can recognize word roots. (p. 54)
WRITING	I can connect sentences with *and* and *but.* (p. 55)
GRAMMAR	I can recognize and use *there is / there are* and *there was / there were.* (p. 56)
LEARNING OUTCOME	I can explain how a place changed because of international immigration or culture.

UNIT 4

Positive Thinking

READING • making inferences
VOCABULARY • phrasal verbs
WRITING • using time order words to write a story
GRAMMAR • simple past

LEARNING OUTCOME

Write about a time when you or someone you know changed a situation with positive thinking.

Unit QUESTION

What are the benefits of positive thinking?

PREVIEW THE UNIT

A Discuss these questions with your classmates.

Do you know someone with a positive way of thinking? Give examples that show this.

Look at the photo. Why is the woman smiling?

B Discuss the Unit Question above with your classmates.

Listen to *The Q Classroom*, Track 11 on CD 1, to hear other answers.

C **Complete the quiz.**

Are You Positive?

Take this quiz. Match these sayings about positive thinking with their explanations.

_e_ **1.** Everyone smiles in the same language. — Unknown	a. Keep trying. Don't give up.
___ **2.** Believe that you will succeed and you will! —The United States	b. Small problems can look big when you are worried.
___ **3.** Fall seven times, stand up eight. — Japan	c. Life is more fun when you try new things.
___ **4.** Since the house is on fire, let's warm ourselves. — Italy	d. Successful people have a lot of confidence.
___ **5.** Nothing is interesting if you're not interested. — Scotland	e. People understand smiling all over the world.
___ **6.** Worry often gives a small thing a big shadow. —Sweden	f. When you have big problems, try to look for the good things

Read these sayings. Check (✓) your favorite saying.

When the sun rises, it rises for everyone.

Let a smile be your umbrella.

Why not learn to enjoy the little things? There are so many of them.

To be a great champion, you need to believe you are the best.

Whenever you fall, pick something up.

D **Discuss the questions in a group.**

1. Which of the sayings above do you like the best? Why?
2. Do you know another saying about positive thinking? Tell your group.
3. Does positive thinking make you happier?

READING 1 | The Power of Positive Thinking?

VOCABULARY

Here are some words from Reading 1. Read their definitions. Then complete each sentence.

attitude (*noun*) the way you think about something
event (*noun*) something important that happens
expect (*verb*) to think something is going to happen
find out (*phrasal verb*) to get information about something
give up (*phrasal verb*) to stop trying to do something
knowledge (*noun*) what you know and understand about something
likely (*adjective*) probably going to happen
work out (*phrasal verb*) to have the result you want

1. I need to ________________ what time the meeting starts. I can't be late!
2. I emailed her yesterday. I ________________ her answer today.
3. He was a good student. His ________________ of English grammar is excellent.
4. I know it's difficult, but don't stop trying. Everything will ________________ in the end.
5. Having a baby was a great ________________ in her life. It changed her in many ways.
6. You need to work hard to be successful. Don't ________________!
7. She never thinks bad thoughts. She has a very positive ________________.
8. Look at those black clouds. I think rain is very ________________.

Preview Reading 1

This is a magazine article about positive thinking.

Preview the reading. Check (✓) your answer.

According to the article, can positive thinking really benefit people?

☐ Yes

☐ No

CD 1 Track 12 **Read the article.**

The Power of Positive Thinking?

1 Positive people are usually happy. They often have a lot of friends. When they have a problem, they try to change the problem into an opportunity. They believe things always **work out**. But can positive thinking really make someone's life better? Many scientists are studying positive thinking. They are **finding out** some very interesting information.

Your Health

2 The Mayo Clinic is a famous medical organization in the United States. It studies many things, including positive thinking. Their research[1] says that positive thinking has many benefits. First, positive thinking supports good health. Positive people don't worry about the bad **events** in life, so they stay healthy. Also, positive people are **likely** to exercise and eat healthy foods. Because of this, they don't usually get sick and don't have many health problems.

At Work

3 Dr. Michael Frese is a professor at the University of Giessen in Germany. His research shows that positive people do well in jobs. There are several reasons for this. Positive people are creative. They don't **expect** other people to help them with problems. They solve problems themselves. And positive people don't **give up**. They keep trying to solve a problem. Positive people also like to learn new things, so they study and take classes. Their new **knowledge** and skills make them better workers.

In Sports

4 Positive thinking helps in sports. Judy McDonald, a researcher at the University of Ottawa, studied successful athletes. Top athletes are positive thinkers. She wrote, "It goes beyond[2] confidence." They never feel like failures[3]. They never give up. They like to practice their sports and always want to get better. Also, before they do an action, they "see" themselves do it correctly. This is called *visualization*. These athletes believe they are going to win.

[1] **research:** a careful study of something to learn new information

[2] **go beyond:** to do more than expected

[3] **failure:** a person who is not successful

Becoming Positive

5 In the past, scientists thought **attitudes** never changed. Now, many psychologists think people can become more positive. There are many different ways to change. Here are some examples. First, think about good events in your life. At the end of a day, ask, "What good things happened to me today?" Think about these things for a few minutes. Second, find fun activities to do. Laugh at a funny movie or read a good book. Finally, always try new things. For example, you can talk to people you don't know or shop in a different store. Do different things every day.

A Good Life

6 Life can be difficult sometimes. Don't give up and be negative. Take action. Think about the future and make a plan. You can learn to be positive.

MAIN IDEAS

Tip for Success

Use a small card to help you pay attention while you read. Place the card at the line you are reading and move it down the page as you read.

Read the statements. Write *T* (true) or *F* (false).

____ 1. Positive people create opportunities for themselves.

____ 2. There is no research on positive thinking.

____ 3. Positive people don't worry about things very much.

____ 4. Positive people often ask for help from other people.

____ 5. Successful athletes believe they can make good things happen.

____ 6. Negative people can become positive people.

DETAILS

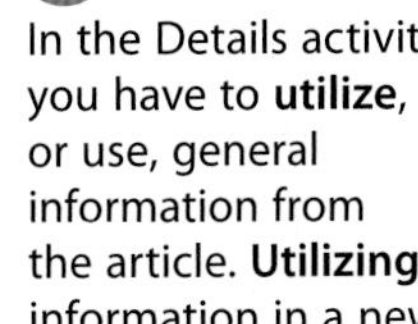

Tip Critical Thinking

In the Details activity, you have to **utilize**, or use, general information from the article. **Utilizing** information in a new situation helps you remember it better.

Read the quotations. According to the article, are these people positive thinkers? Check (✓) the positive quotes.

☐ 1. "I have a lot of problems, but things always work out."
☐ 2. "I can't sleep before an important event."
☐ 3. "It was a bad job, but I learned some important things."
☐ 4. "I plan to take a class at the university very soon."
☐ 5. "I like soccer, but sometimes I don't want to practice."
☐ 6. "I have a meeting today. I believe it will go well."
☐ 7. "I like to do the same things every day."
☐ 8. "There are so many interesting people to meet."

Reading Skill | Making inferences 

Writers do not always give information directly. They want you to understand their meaning without stating it directly. An **inference** is a guess about something that is not stated in the reading. You make inferences, or look at the information, and decide what is true. Good readers make inferences all the time. Here are some examples of inferences.

Statement: "I'm happy to be alive after that accident."
Inference: The accident was very serious.

Statement: "I never believed in positive thinking until today."
Inference: Something good happened to this person.

Statement: "My soccer team lost all of its games. Then we tried positive thinking."
Inference: Now the team is winning some games.

A. Read Reading 1 again. Circle the best inference for each section of the article.

1. Your Health
   a. Positive people usually live longer than negative people.
   b. We need more information about positive thinking and health.
2. At Work
   a. It's difficult for positive people to work with negative people.
   b. Successful businesspeople are usually positive people.
3. In Sports
   a. Great athletes lose many of their games.
   b. Great athletes work hard for their success.
4. Becoming Positive
   a. Good thoughts can change bad attitudes.
   b. Bad things never happen to positive people.

B. Which statements do you think the writer of Reading 1 agrees with? Check (✓) your inferences.

☐ 1. Next time you're in a group, talk to a person you don't know.
☐ 2. Every day, think about something you did badly.
☐ 3. When you have a difficult problem, ask for help right away.
☐ 4. It's important to eat fresh fruit and vegetables.

What Do You Think?

Complete the activities in a group.

1. How positive are you? Put an *X* on the line to show how positive you are. Think of stories or examples that show this and tell your group.

How positive are you?

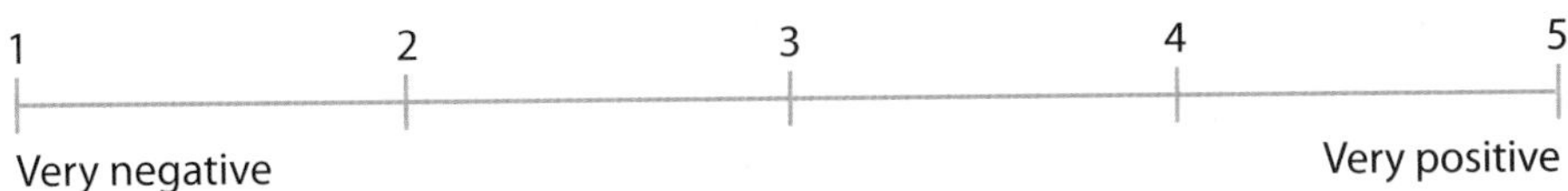

2. The article says that these things are true about positive people. Are they true about you? Check (✓) *Yes* or *No*. Discuss your answers in a group.

	Yes	No
a. I know many different people.	☐	☐
b. I eat healthy food and get a lot of exercise.	☐	☐
c. I don't worry about things very much.	☐	☐
d. I like to solve problems myself.	☐	☐
e. I like to learn new things.	☐	☐
f. I work hard because success is always possible.	☐	☐
g. I expect things to go well.	☐	☐
h. I think about good events in my life.	☐	☐
i. I think about my future in a positive way.	☐	☐

3. Choose two true statements from the chart in Activity 2. Write them in your notebook, and write an example for each statement.

I like to learn new things. I plan to study the Chinese language next year.

READING 2 | The Lost Horse

VOCABULARY

Here are some words from Reading 2. Read their definitions. Then complete each sentence.

farm (*noun*) land and buildings where people keep animals and grow plants for food
government (*noun*) the group of people who officially rule or control a country
nation (*noun*) a country and all the people who live in it
run away (*phrasal verb*) to go quickly away from a place
send (*verb*) to make someone or something go somewhere
war (*noun*) fighting between countries or between groups of people
wild (*adjective*) living or growing in nature, not with humans
wise (*adjective*) knowing and understanding a lot about many things

1. The countries decided to end the ________________ and be friendly neighbors.
2. My grandmother helps me make good decisions. She is very ________________.
3. We keep the cat in the house all the time. It cannot ________________.
4. They grow vegetables on their ________________.
5. The animal was ________________. It never saw people.
6. The ________________ of the United States is in Washington, D.C.
7. Ethiopia is an African ________________. It has a population of 80 million.
8. Every summer, Dan and Alice ________________ their children to summer school.

Preview Reading 2

This is an old story from China. It teaches a lesson about positive and negative thinking.

Look at the three pictures. What events happen in the story? Do you think they are good or bad events?

CD 1 Track 13 **Read the story.**

The Lost Horse

1 A **wise** old man and his son lived on a small **farm**. They had just one horse. One day the horse **ran away**. All the farmer's neighbors said, "What bad news! Your horse ran away!" The farmer said, "Bad news? Good news? Who knows?"

2 A month later, the farmer's horse came back to the farm with a **wild** horse. All the farmer's neighbors said, "What good news! Now you have two horses!" The farmer said, "Good news? Bad news? Who knows?"

3 The next day, the farmer and the boy decided to use the wild horse for farm work. The farmer's son tried to ride the wild horse. He fell and broke his leg. All the farmer's neighbors said, "What bad news! Your son is hurt." The farmer said, "Bad news? Good news? Who knows?"

4 Then a **war** started between the farmer's **nation** and its neighbor. The **government** needed all the country's young men to fight in the war. Men from the government came to town. They took all the healthy young men, but they didn't **send** the farmer's boy to war. His leg was broken. Many of the young men from the town died in the war. After several months, the boy's leg got better. All the farmer's neighbors said, "What good news! Your son didn't go to war, and now he is healthy!" The farmer said, "Good news? Bad news? Who knows?"

MAIN IDEAS

Circle the answer to each question.

1. Who doesn't think news is good or bad?
   a. the neighbors
   b. the wise old man
   c. the son

2. What does the story try to teach us?
   a. Good news always follows bad news when you have a positive attitude.
   b. When you don't have a positive attitude, good things can still happen.
   c. Good news can become bad news. Bad news can become good news.

DETAILS

A. Read the sentences. Order the details from the story (1–6).

____ a. The country went to war.

____ b. The horse came back with a wild horse.

____ c. The men from the government didn't send the boy to war.

__1__ d. The horse ran away from the farm.

____ e. The boy fell off the wild horse.

____ f. The boy got healthy again.

B. What inferences can you make about the old man? Read the story again. Check (✓) the inferences.

____ 1. He doesn't talk a lot.

____ 2. He has a big family.

____ 3. He is poor.

____ 4. He worries about the future.

____ 5. He has only one son.

____ 6. His neighbors care about him.

____ 7. He has or had a wife.

____ 8. He has an easy life.

WHAT DO YOU THINK?

A. Discuss the questions in a group.

1. The wise old man in Reading 2 knew that bad events sometimes follow good events. What is a possible bad event to follow this good event? Good event: You win a lot of money.
2. The wise old man also knew that good events sometimes follow bad events. What is a possible good event to follow this bad event? Bad event: You miss the bus to work one Monday.

B. Think about both Reading 1 and Reading 2 as you discuss the questions.

1. In your opinion, is the old man in Reading 2 a positive thinker? Give reasons and examples for your opinion.
2. How are positive thinkers different from negative thinkers?

Vocabulary Skill | Phrasal verbs

Most **phrasal verbs** have two words. The first word is the *verb*. The second word is either a short *adverb* or a *preposition*. The two words together have a different meaning from the verb alone.

look (*verb*) to use your eyes to see

look after (*phrasal verb*) to take care of someone or something

look for (*phrasal verb*) to try to find someone or something

look out (*phrasal verb*) to be careful or pay attention

look through (*phrasal verb*) to read something quickly

Look where you are going!
Debra **looks after** her little sister on weekends.
I'm **looking for** my notebook. I can't find it.
Look out! There's a hole in the sidewalk.
Let's **look through** this furniture catalog.

Phrasal verbs are very common in writing and speech. Learn phrasal verbs to improve your understanding when you read.

A. **Work with a partner. Match each phrasal verb with its definition. You may use a dictionary to help you.**

___	1. speak up	a. visit
___	2. give up	b. to become less afraid or excited
___	3. calm down	c. to talk louder
___	4. slow down	d. to get information about something
___	5. find out	e. to start to move more slowly
___	6. come over	f. to stop trying to do something

B. **Read the sentences. Complete each sentence with the correct phrasal verb from Activity A. Then compare your answers with your partner.**

1. Could you please ________________? I can't hear you.
2. Do you want to ________________ for dinner at our house tonight?
3. I can't figure out this difficult math problem. I'm going to ________________.
4. John was very nervous before the exam, so he took a walk to help him ________________.
5. Mirabel is calling the restaurant to ________________ if they are open on Monday.
6. You're driving too fast. You need to ________________ or you might get a ticket.

C. **Choose five phrasal verbs from Activity A and write a sentence for each.**

1. ____
2. ____
3. ____
4. ____
5. ____

WRITING

Grammar Simple past

Regular verbs

Use the **simple past** to talk about actions that happened in the past.

- To form the simple past of regular verbs, add *-ed* to the base form of the verb.

I expect**ed** the good news. I listen**ed** to my friend.

- For verbs ending in *e*, just add *-d*.

I serve**d** lunch and dinner at a busy restaurant. I also prepare**d** takeout orders.

- For verbs ending in *y*, drop the *y* and add *-ied*.

Tom appl**ied** for a position as a website designer. He stud**ied** art and computers in college.

Irregular verbs

- The verb *be* is irregular in the simple past. It has two forms: *was* and *were*.

My internship **was** a good experience. The people **were** great.

- Here are some common irregular verbs with their simple past forms.

come	**came**	go	**went**	make	**made**	take	**took**
do	**did**	have	**had**	say	**said**		
get	**got**	know	**knew**	see	**saw**		

Negative forms of the simple past

To form a negative statement, use *did* + *not* (or *didn't*) + base form of the verb.

I **didn't graduate** from high school last year. It was two years ago.

A. Look back at Reading 2. Underline the simple past forms of these verbs in the story. Then write the simple past forms.

1. break ________________
2. come ________________
3. fall ________________
4. get ________________
5. have ________________
6. run ________________
7. say ________________
8. send ________________
9. take ________________

B. **Complete each sentence with the simple past form of a verb from the box. Use one verb two times.**

have	lose	go	run	say	take

1. Nancy ________________ to school in the city.
2. She ________________ the train to school every day.
3. One day, she ________________ a bag of school papers in her hand.
4. A person ________________ her bag and ________________ out the door.
5. She ________________ all of her homework papers.
6. She ________________, "Now I can't do my homework!"

Tip for Success

Many verbs have irregular past forms. Dictionaries usually show the simple past form.

Writing Skill | Using time order words to write a story

When we write a story, we often use **time order words** to show the order of events. Time order words tell the reader what happens first, second, third, and so on. Here are the time order words in the story "The Lost Horse."

One day, the horse ran away.
A month later, the horse came back.
The next day, the farmer decided to use the wild horse for farm work.
Then a war started.
After several months, the boy's leg got better.

Note: Write a comma after time order words at the beginning of a sentence. Short introductory words or phrases sometimes do not need a comma.

A. **Read the story. Underline the time order words.**

Winning by Losing

I'm a tennis player. I play in important tennis matches. In the beginning, I was lazy and I didn't practice. One day, I lost badly. I was very angry because I loved tennis. The next day, I started to exercise. I ate healthy food, and I practiced tennis every day. After several months, I was strong and fast. I won some games. Tennis became my life. One year later, I won an important tennis match. Now I'm an excellent athlete. I'm very happy that I lost in the beginning. That bad event changed my attitude.

A story always has a title. All the words start with capital letters, except for prepositions (*in*, *at*, *on*), articles (*a*, *the*), and conjunctions (*and*, *or*). The first word is always capitalized.

B. Complete the story with the time order words from the box.

after	first	later	next	then

Changing a Problem into an Opportunity

My mother worked in a restaurant. ________(1) five years, the restaurant closed. She was sad about this bad event for a little while. ________(2), she made a plan. ________(3), she borrowed money from our family. ________(4), she opened a small restaurant downtown. She worked long hours in the restaurant. Business was bad sometimes, but she didn't give up. Three years ________(5), her restaurant was a success. My mother's hard work changed her problem into an opportunity.

Unit Assignment | Write a story about positive thinking

In this assignment, you are going to write about a time that you or someone you know changed a bad event to a good event with positive thinking. As you write, think about the Unit Question, "What are the benefits of positive thinking?" and refer to the Self-Assessment checklist on page 76.

For alternative unit assignments, see the *Q: Skills for Success Teacher's Handbook*.

PLAN AND WRITE

A. BRAINSTORM Complete the activities.

1. Work with a partner or in a group. Take turns telling about a time you or someone you know changed a bad event to a good event with positive thinking.
2. Decide which story you want to write about. You can write about yourself, or someone you know, or a classmate.

B. PLAN Organize your story. Answer the questions.

1. Who is the story about? ________________________________

2. Where was it? ___________________________________

3. What happened first? ___________________________________

4. What happened next? ___________________________________

5. What happened after that? ___________________________________

C. WRITE Write your story in your notebook. Remember to include a title, write in the simple past, and use time order words. Look at the Self-Assessment checklist below to guide your writing.

Revise and Edit

A. PEER REVIEW Read a partner's story. Answer the questions and discuss them with your partner.

1. Is this a story about positive thinking?
2. What time order words does your partner use? Circle all the time words.
3. Does your partner tell the story in the simple past? Underline all the simple past verb forms.
4. Is there something you don't understand? Write a question mark (?) in the margin.

B. REWRITE Review the answers to the questions in Activity A. You may want to revise and rewrite your story.

C. EDIT Complete the Self-Assessment checklist as you prepare to write the final draft of your story. Be prepared to hand in your work or discuss it in class.

SELF-ASSESSMENT		
Yes	No	
☐	☐	Does the story have a title?
☐	☐	Does every sentence begin with a capital letter?
☐	☐	Does every sentence have final punctuation?
☐	☐	Does every sentence have a subject and a verb?
☐	☐	Does every subject and verb agree?
☐	☐	Is the spelling correct? Check a dictionary if you are not sure.
☐	☐	Does the story have vocabulary words from the unit?
☐	☐	Is the use of the simple past correct?
☐	☐	Is the use of time order words correct?

Track Your Success

Circle the words you learned in this unit.

Nouns	**Verbs**	**Adjectives**
attitude 🔑 AWL	expect 🔑	likely 🔑
event 🔑	find out 🔑	wild 🔑
farm 🔑	give up	wise
government 🔑	run away	
knowledge 🔑	send 🔑	
nation 🔑	work out	
war 🔑		

🔑 Oxford 2000 keywords

AWL Academic Word List

Check (✓) the skills you learned. If you need more work on a skill, refer to the page(s) in parentheses.

READING	I can make inferences. (p. 66)
VOCABULARY	I can recognize and use phrasal verbs. (p. 71)
WRITING	I can recognize and use the simple past. (p. 73)
GRAMMAR	I can use time order words to write a story. (p. 74)
LEARNING OUTCOME	I can write about a time when I or someone I know changed a situation with positive thinking.

UNIT 5

Vacation

READING	reading charts, graphs, and tables
VOCABULARY	compound nouns
WRITING	using correct paragraph structure
GRAMMAR	sentences with *because*

LEARNING OUTCOME

Write a paragraph explaining how much vacation time you need.

Unit QUESTION

Why is vacation important?

PREVIEW THE UNIT

A Discuss these questions with your classmates.

How much vacation do schoolchildren have each year?

Which jobs give more vacation time? Which jobs give less?

Look at the photo. What is the man doing? How do you think he feels?

B Discuss the Unit Question above with your classmates.

Listen to *The Q Classroom*, Track 14 on CD 1, to hear other answers.

C Work with a partner. Look at the photos. Which vacation activities do you like best? Take turns telling your partner about your favorite activities.

going to the beach

hiking in the mountains

visiting famous places

visiting family

D Complete the chart for yourself and a partner.

	Me	My Partner
1. How often do you take a vacation?		
2. How long is your vacation usually?		
3. What do you do on vacation?		
4. Who do you go on vacation with?		

READING 1 | Vacation from Work

VOCABULARY

Here are some words from Reading 1. Read the paragraphs. Then write each bold word next to the correct definition.

Toys Inc. is a small toy company. It **produces** beautiful wooden toys. There are 45 **employees** at Toys Inc. They work hard to make the toys. The employees have difficult **schedules**. Some work 12 hours a day. Some work all night.

wooden toys

The president of the company knows that long hours of hard work can be difficult and can cause **stress**. For this reason, she plans to change the vacation **policy**. Now employees work 50 weeks. She wants to **reduce** the number of weeks they work to 48. She wants to give the employees more time to rest and spend time with their families. The company wants to **improve** the lives of its employees. Happy workers are important to a company's success.

Tip for Success

Look at each new word and ask yourself: *What part of speech is it? Is it a noun, verb, etc.?*

1. ________________ (*noun*) a feeling of being very worried because of problems in your life
2. ________________ (*verb*) to become better or to make something better
3. ________________ (*verb*) to make or grow something
4. ________________ (*noun*) the plans of a government, organization, or company
5. ________________ (*noun*) a person who works for someone
6. ________________ (*noun*) a list that shows when something happens
7. ________________ (*verb*) to make something smaller or less

PREVIEW READING 1

You are going to read an email from the president of Toys Inc. to the employees about the company's vacation policy.

Scan the email, including the chart on page 83. Answer the questions.

1. What is the problem at Toys Inc.? ________________
2. What does the email ask employees to do? ________________

CD 1 Track 15 **Read the email.**

From: Christine Drake, President
To: All **employees** of Toys Inc.
Subject: Toys Inc. Employee Vacation **Policy**

Toys Inc. wants its **employees** to be happy and successful. I feel it is important for all employees to take vacation, yet many of you do not take enough vacation. Some of you do not take any vacation. I want everyone to take time off.

There are two options[1] for you to look at. I ask you to choose one of the two options. One option gives reasons to keep our current vacation policy. The other option gives reasons to change our current policy and close the business for two weeks every year.

Please read about the two options and reasons for each. Then check (✔) the option you like best. Please return your email with your choice by the end of the day Friday.

OPTION 1 (**POLICY** NOW): ☐   OPTION 2 (NEW POLICY): ☐

OPTION 1: KEEP CURRENT VACATION POLICY

Now, at Toys Inc., all employees have two weeks of vacation every year. Employees choose when to use their vacation days. Here are some reasons to keep the policy we have now.

- Employees can use their vacation time anytime. They can plan a vacation around their family needs.
- Closing the factory for two weeks **reduces** the number of toys we **produce**. We don't want to lose business. Other factories are open 52 weeks a year. We need to do the same.
- The company can reduce worker **stress** in other ways. We can give our workers a place to exercise so they can **improve** their health. We can give our employees special **schedules** or reduce the hours they work. We do not need to close the company just because some workers need to take a vacation.

[1] **option:** a thing you can choose

OPTION 2: CHANGE THE VACATION POLICY

One way for all employees to take vacation is to close our business for two weeks every year. All employees take their vacation during those two weeks. Here are some reasons to change this policy.

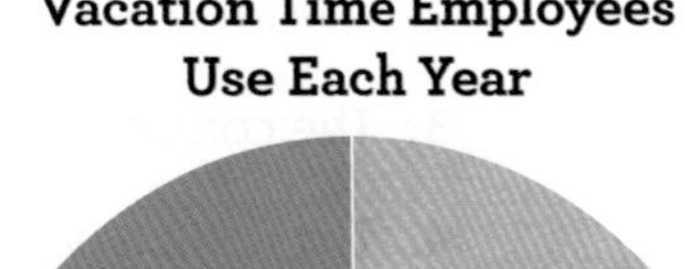

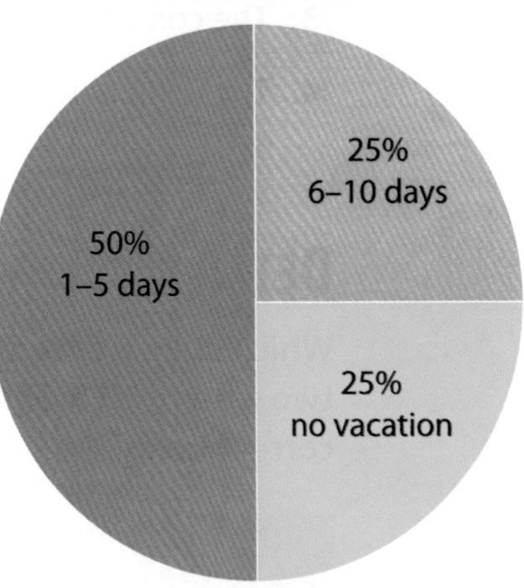

Source: Toys Inc. Department of Human Resources

- Our employees do not take the vacation time they need. Some employees don't take vacations at all. Many employees *do* go on vacation, but they don't stop thinking about work. They call the company during their vacation. They check their company email. Closing the company every year for two weeks solves this problem.
- It works in other countries. In China, companies give their employees a week of vacation called Golden Week. Everyone takes a vacation at the same time.
- Tired workers lose money for the company. Many of our employees work long hours. They are more likely to have accidents and get hurt. They are more likely to feel stress and get sick. Every time an employee gets hurt or sick, we produce less.
- Vacations are good for business because they are good for employees. Vacations improve the work employees do. Vacations improve worker attention. Vacations improve worker health. Healthy and happy employees produce more.

Main Ideas

Tip for Success

Underline the most important information in a reading text. After you read the text, study the parts you underlined. This helps you remember the information in the text.

Do these statements describe the Toys Inc. vacation policy now (Option 1) or the possible new policy (Option 2)? Check (✓) the correct box.

	Option 1	Option 2
1. The employees take their vacation anytime.	☐	☐
2. The employees take their vacation at the same time.	☐	☐
3. The company closes for two weeks.	☐	☐
4. The company stays open all year long.	☐	☐

Details

Which statements are reasons *for* the change (closing the company for two weeks)? Which statements are *against* the change? Check (✓) the correct box.

	For Change	Against Change
1. Employees can plan vacations around their families.	☐	☐
2. Toys Inc. can change schedules and reduce the number of hours employees work.	☐	☐
3. Toys Inc. workers don't take enough vacation.	☐	☐
4. Closing the office for two weeks reduces the number of toys Toys Inc. produces.	☐	☐
5. Many workers are tired and more likely to have accidents.	☐	☐
6. Many workers check their work email during their vacation.	☐	☐

Reading Skill | Reading charts, graphs, and tables

Many texts you read have **charts**, **graphs**, or **tables** in them. Charts, graphs, and tables are very useful because they give a lot of information in a small space. They also make it easier to understand a text.

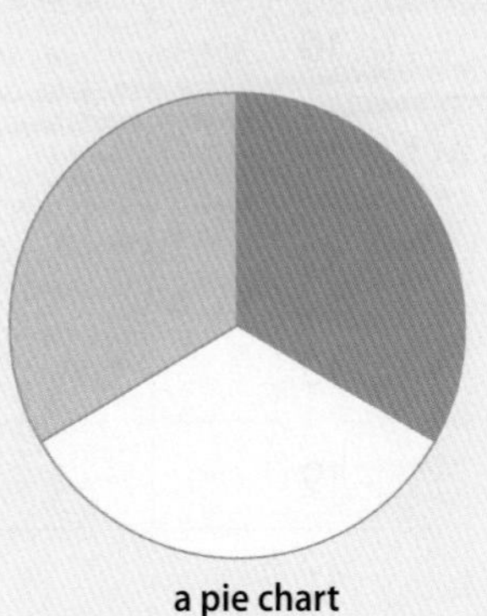

a pie chart

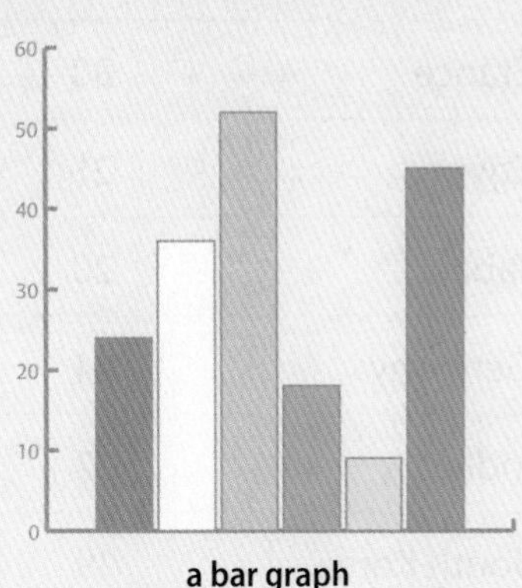

a bar graph

	XXXXX	XXXXX
1		
2		
3		
4		

a chart or table

It's important to look at charts when you *preview*, *skim*, and *scan* a text. Here are some tips.

- Read the title and headings to get the main idea.
- Look at the numbers. To find details, scan for only the numbers that you want to know about.

Tip Critical Thinking

Activity A and Activity B both ask you to **interpret** a table or a graph. To interpret, you have to take information in one form and change it into another form. In A and B, you have to use numbers to understand ideas.

A. Look at the table and answer the questions.

Vacations and Holidays Around the World			
Countries	**Vacation Days**	**Holidays**	**Total Days Off**
Finland	30	14	44
France	30	10	40
Egypt	21	16	37
Japan	20	15	35
Germany	24	10	34
India	12	19	31
South Korea	19	11	30
Singapore	14	12	26
United States	15	10	25
Vietnam	14	8	22

1. What is the title? ______________________
2. What are the four headings?

   ______________ ______________

   ______________ ______________

3. This chart is part of a magazine article. What do you think the article is about? (What is its main idea?)

   ____
4. Which country has 44 total days off from work? ______________
5. Which countries have only 10 holidays? ______________
6. How many holidays do workers in India get? ______________
7. How many vacation days do workers in Egypt get? ______________
8. Which country has the lowest number of days off from work?

   ____

B. **Look at the bar graph and answer the questions.**

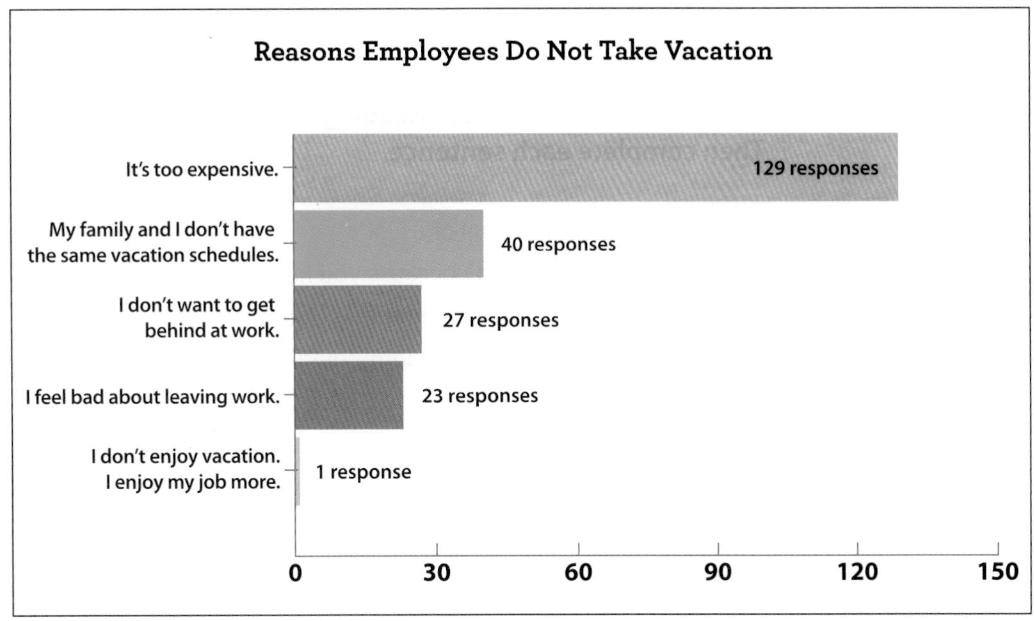

1. What is the title? ______________________________

2. What is the number-one reason people do not take vacation?

   ____

3. How many people don't enjoy vacation? ______________________________

4. How many people cannot take vacation at the same time as their family? ______________

WHAT DO YOU THINK?

Discuss the questions in a group. Then choose one question and write two or three sentences about it in your notebook.

1. Are you for or against the change in vacation policy for Toys Inc.? Why? Use a reason from Reading 1 to support your answer.
2. What is the vacation policy for your school or work? Explain it.

READING 2 | Vacation from School

VOCABULARY

Here are some words from Reading 2. Read their definitions. Then complete each sentence.

average (*adjective*) normal or usual
bored (*adjective*) unhappy because you have nothing interesting to do
compete (*verb*) to try to do better than someone else
discover (*verb*) to find or learn something for the first time
experience (*noun*) knowledge you have from doing something again and again
relax (*verb*) to rest and be calm
review (*verb*) to study something again to remember it or understand it

1. Families are very busy all the time. There is no time to slow down and ________________.
2. The two football teams ________________ against each other. They both want to win.
3. My children learn a lot in school, but it's all book learning. They don't have much ________________ in the world.
4. Before a test, students ________________ the information they learned.
5. In the United States, the ________________ summer vacation for schoolchildren is 11 weeks.
6. Many children are ________________ in the summer because they have nothing to do.
7. The world is new to young children. Every day, they ________________ something new.

PREVIEW READING 2

You are going to read two letters from people in the town of Waterville to their local newspaper. Often people in a town write letters to the newspaper to say what they think about different town policies or plans. The town of Waterville needs to decide what to do about vacation for schoolchildren.

Skim the two letters and answer the questions.

1. Which person is *for* a long school vacation? ____________

2. Which person is *against* it? ____________

CD 1 Track 16 **Read the letters to the editor.**

Letters to the Editor

Yes to a Longer School Year

To the Editor:

1 Why do our children have 11 weeks of summer vacation? Many years ago, 85 percent of Americans worked on farms. Children needed summer vacation because they helped with the farm work. Today, only 3 percent of Americans work on farms. But our children still have long summer vacations. We have to change the school schedule.

2 American students lose between one and two months of learning during their summer vacations. We call this "summer learning loss." Away from school for so many weeks, students forget what they learned. Experts[1] say that students lose math skills and reading skills. At the beginning of school in September, teachers need to **review** last year's studies for the first four to six weeks of school. This is not a good use of classroom time.

Summer vacations are not great opportunities for learning. Most parents work outside of the home. They cannot be with their kids[2] during the long summer months. Some families can pay for summer camps[3], but many cannot. Most children stay home and watch TV. They are **bored**. Most children do not learn new skills during the summer.

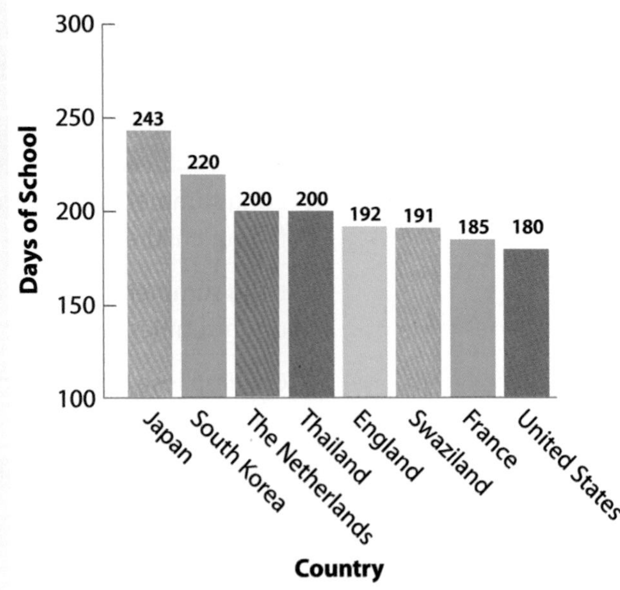

[1] **expert:** a person who knows a lot about something
[2] **kid:** a child or teenager
[3] **summer camp:** a place with sports and learning activities where children live during the summer months

3 Students in the United States do not have a high number of school days. Many other countries have more. The **average** number of school days in Japan is 243. In the United States, the average number is only 180. Our children need more school time and less vacation time. Then they can **compete** in the world today.

James Walsh, Teacher

Lincoln Elementary School, Waterville

Vacations Are a Way of Learning

To the Editor:

1 I am against a longer school year. I believe people learn everywhere, not just in school. I believe children need **experience** in the world.

2 Summer vacation is a great opportunity. Kids can **discover** the world outside of school. They can learn to do things they can't learn in a classroom. They can learn to swim and ride bikes. They can travel or go to summer camps. They can take time to do things like cooking and art. Some can get summer jobs. They can get work experience or help people in the community. They can spend time with people of other ages. Basically, they can get more experience in the world.

3 Long summer vacations give families time together. During the school year, everyone is busy. During summer vacations, we learn to **relax**. We take time to do things together. Vacations are good for families.

Linda Smith, Parent

Waterville schools

MAIN IDEAS

Read the two letters again. Which are main ideas of James Walsh's letter? Which are main ideas of Linda Smith's letter? Check (✓) the box.

	James Walsh	Linda Smith
1. Long summer vacations are not necessary for our children today.	☐	☐
2. Long summer vacations are great learning opportunities.	☐	☐
3. Children lose learning skills over the long summer vacation.	☐	☐
4. It is not a good idea for the town to change the vacation rules.	☐	☐

DETAILS

A. Circle the answer that best completes each statement.

1. James Walsh says that, many years ago, most children used their vacation time to ______.
   a. work on the farm
   b. go to summer camps
   c. have new experiences

2. James Walsh says most parents ______ during the summer months.
   a. travel
   b. are with their children
   c. work

3. Linda Smith says children can get ______ during their summer vacations.
   a. better math skills
   b. work experience
   c. more classroom time

4. Linda Smith thinks children need ______.
   a. experience outside of school
   b. more time to sleep
   c. many vacations during the year

B. Look at the bar graph in the reading text and answer the questions.

1. How many days of school do children in Swaziland have? ____________
2. How many days of school do children in France have? ______________
3. How many days of school do children in Thailand have? ____________
4. Which country has 243 school days? _________________
5. Which country has 220 school days? _________________
6. Which country has 180 school days? _________________

What Do You Think?

A. Discuss the questions in a group.

1. When you were a kid, how much vacation time did you have from school? Did you need more or less time?
2. What did you do on your vacations? What kinds of things did you learn on your vacations?

B. Think about both Reading 1 and Reading 2 as you discuss the questions.

1. Are long summer vacations necessary for children? Why or why not?
2. Do children need more vacation time than adults? Why or why not?

Vocabulary Skill | Compound nouns

We often put two nouns together to form a **compound noun**. The first noun describes the second noun. It acts like an adjective.

classroom time = time in a classroom
family needs = needs of a family
summer vacation = vacation during the summer

Knowing how to use compound nouns correctly increases your vocabulary and helps you sound more natural.

When a noun acts like an adjective, it cannot be plural.

✓ classroom time
✗ classrooms time

✓ family needs
✗ families needs

A. Change each phrase into a compound noun.

1. experience in life = ___life experience___
2. experience in work = ______________
3. time for relaxation = ______________

4. time for work = ______________________

5. stress in a job = ______________________

6. stress in families = ______________________

7. program in a school = ______________________

8. program for math = ______________________

9. activity in the summer = ______________________

10. activities at a school = ______________________

11. rules for a school = ______________________

12. rules for vacations = ______________________

B. Order the words. Write a question.

1. school / What / your / schedule / is

   What is your school schedule______________________?

2. your / school / How long / is / year

   ______________________?

3. month / your favorite / Which is / summer

   ______________________?

4. on / summer / What do / do / your / vacation / you

   ______________________?

5. have / work / What kind of / do you / experience

   ______________________?

6. teenagers / experiences / What kind of / life / do / need

   ______________________?

C. Compare your answers for Activity B with a partner. Then take turns asking and answering the questions.

WRITING

Writing Skill Using correct paragraph structure 

A **paragraph** is a group of sentences about one main idea. Paragraphs for school and university work usually have the following parts.

- **A topic sentence:** This sentence tells the main idea of the whole paragraph. It is usually the first or second sentence in the paragraph.
- **Supporting sentences:** These sentences explain the main idea. They often give examples and details.
- **A concluding sentence:** This sentence ends the paragraph. Sometimes it tells the reader the main idea again. Some paragraphs, especially short ones, do not have a concluding sentence.

A strong paragraph is important for good writing.

Note: At the beginning of a paragraph, the writer indents the first line. This means the line starts after five letter spaces.

A. Read the paragraph. Underline the topic sentence, the three supporting sentences, and the concluding sentence. Then write *TS* (topic sentence), *SS* (supporting sentence), or *CS* (concluding sentence) above each sentence.

TS

Vacations are not the right answer to worker stress. First of all, one or two vacations a year cannot reduce the stress of many days of long work hours. Also, vacations can actually be very stressful because they are expensive and difficult. Finally, people lived for thousands of years without vacations. Vacations are not necessary.

B. **Read the sentences about the Chinese vacation policy for Golden Week. Put them into the order of a paragraph. Number them 1–5.**

___ Finally, with the Golden Week policy, a worker is sure to have a vacation with pay every year.

___ First of all, many Chinese people work far away from their hometowns, and Golden Week gives them enough time to travel back home.

___ For these three reasons, the Golden Week policy is a good idea.

___ Many people in China like the Golden Week vacation policy because it improves workers' lives in the following ways.

___ Also, the Golden Week policy makes it easy to plan a big family party because everyone has a vacation at the same time.

C. **Write the sentences in Activity B in the form of a paragraph in your notebook. Remember to indent the first line.**

Grammar Sentences with *because*

web

You can combine two sentences with *because*. *Because* introduces the reason for a situation or state.

Bob is a doctor. (reason) → He cannot take long vacations. (situation)
Bob cannot take long vacations **because** he is a doctor.
Because Bob is a doctor, he cannot take long vacations.

I worked many hours yesterday. (reason) → I am tired. (state)
I am tired **because** I worked many hours yesterday.
Because I worked many hours yesterday, I am tired.

- There is no comma when *because* is in the middle of the sentence. There is a comma when the sentence begins with *because*.
- When the subject in both parts of the sentence is the same, use a pronoun in the second part of the sentence.

✓ **Lucy** is tired because **she** worked many hours yesterday.
✗ **Lucy** is tired because **Lucy** worked many hours yesterday.

A. Write two sentences with *because*. Remember that *because* introduces the reason.

1. People need a break from work. → People take vacations.

   a. People take vacations because they need a break from work.

   b. Because people need a break from work, they take vacations.

2. Truck drivers work long hours. → They have a lot of job stress.

   a. ______________________

   b. ______________________

3. Some employees don't have paid vacation. → Some employees don't take vacations.

   a. ______________________

   b. ______________________

4. Some employees have family needs. → Some employees have special schedules.

   a. ______________________

   b. ______________________

5. Children spend all their time in school. → Children don't learn about the world.

   a. ______________________

   b. ______________________

B. Complete each sentence with your own idea. Read your sentences to a partner.

1. I like to go on vacation in the summer because ______________________

   ____

2. Today, people have a lot of work stress because ______________________

   ____

Unit Assignment | Write a paragraph giving reasons

In this assignment, you are going to write a paragraph in which you answer the question, "How much vacation do you need?" As you prepare your paragraph, think about the Unit Question, "Why is vacation important?" and refer to the Self-Assessment checklist on page 98.

For alternative unit assignments, see the *Q: Skills for Success Teacher's Handbook*.

PLAN AND WRITE

A. BRAINSTORM Complete the activities.

1. Discuss the question with a partner. How many vacation days do you need in a year? Why do you need that number of vacation days?
2. Think about what you want and need to do during your vacation. Write four reasons in your notebook.

   I need to spend time with my family.

3. Choose the three best reasons. You will use them in Activity B.

Tip for Success

The commas in the sentences in Activity B all come after an introductory word or phrase (*First of all, Finally, For these three reasons*). Remember to use commas after the phrases.

B. PLAN Write your ideas. Complete the sentences.

Topic sentence: I need ______ vacation days each year.

Reason 1: First of all, I need ______ vacation days because

____.

Reason 2: I also need them because ____________________

____.

Reason 3: Finally, I really need that many days because ____________

____.

Concluding sentence: For these three reasons, I need at least ______ vacation days.

C. WRITE Write your paragraph in your notebook. Remember to indent the first line. Look at the Self-Assessment checklist on page 98 to guide your writing.

Revise and Edit

A. PEER REVIEW Read a partner's paragraph. Answer the questions and discuss them with your partner.

1. Is there a topic sentence? Write *TS* next to the topic sentence.
2. Are there three reasons? Write *SS* next to supporting sentences.
3. Is there a concluding sentence? Write *CS* next to the concluding sentence.
4. Is there something you don't understand? Write a question mark (?) in the margin.

B. REWRITE Review the answers to the questions in Activity A. You may want to revise and rewrite your paragraph.

C. EDIT Complete the Self-Assessment checklist as you prepare to write the final draft of your paragraph. Be prepared to hand in your work or discuss it in class.

SELF-ASSESSMENT		
Yes	No	
☐	☐	Is the first line of the paragraph indented?
☐	☐	Does every sentence begin with a capital letter?
☐	☐	Does every sentence have final punctuation?
☐	☐	Does every sentence have a subject and a verb?
☐	☐	Does every subject and verb agree?
☐	☐	Is the spelling correct? Check a dictionary if you are not sure.
☐	☐	Does the paragraph have vocabulary words from the unit?
☐	☐	Is the use of *because* correct?

Track Your Success

Circle the words you learned in this unit.

Nouns	**Verbs**	**Adjectives**
employee	compete	average 🔑
experience 🔑	discover 🔑	bored 🔑
policy AWL	improve 🔑	
schedule 🔑 AWL	produce 🔑	
stress 🔑 AWL	reduce 🔑	
	relax 🔑 AWL	
	review	

🔑 Oxford 2000 keywords

AWL Academic Word List

Check (✓) the skills you learned. If you need more work on a skill, refer to the page(s) in parentheses.

READING	I can read charts, graphs, and tables. (p. 85)
VOCABULARY	I can recognize and use compound nouns. (p. 92)
WRITING	I can use correct paragraph structure. (p. 94)
GRAMMAR	I can write sentences with *because.* (p. 95)
LEARNING OUTCOME	I can write a paragraph explaining how much vacation time I need.

UNIT 6

Laughter

READING • identifying the topic sentence in a paragraph
VOCABULARY • using the dictionary
GRAMMAR • sentences with *when*
WRITING • writing a topic sentence

LEARNING OUTCOME

Explain what makes you or someone you know laugh.

Unit QUESTION

What makes you laugh?

PREVIEW THE UNIT

A **Discuss these questions with your classmates.**

Do you laugh often?

What kind of laugh do you have? Is it loud or quiet?

Look at the photo. Why are the women laughing?

B **Discuss the Unit Question above with your classmates.**

Listen to *The Q Classroom*, Track 2 on CD 2, to hear other answers.

C **Look at the photos below. Why do you think each person is laughing? Write your idea for each photo. Then discuss your ideas in a group.**

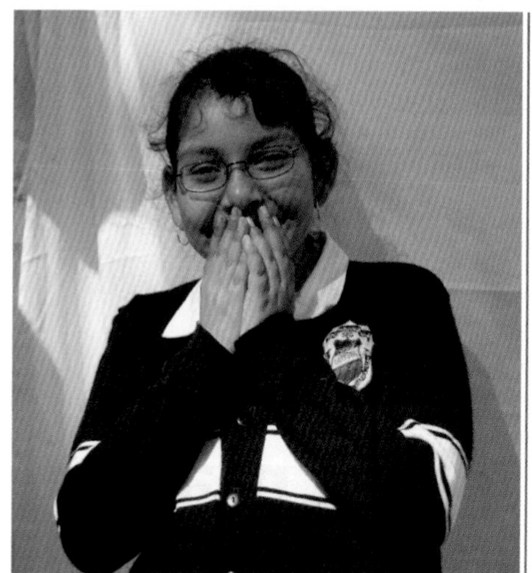

1. ____________________ 2. ____________________

3. ____________________ 4. ____________________

D **Discuss the questions with your group.**

1. Do you laugh for the same reasons as the people in the pictures?
2. Tell the group about a time you laughed a lot. Why did you laugh?

READING

READING 1 | What Is Laughter?

VOCABULARY

Tip for Success

Many adjectives have the same form as verbs in the simple past, for example, *surprised* and *embarrassed*.

Here are some words from Reading 1. Read the sentences. Then write each bold word next to the correct definition.

1. I think laughter is **natural**, just like eating and sleeping.
2. I don't really like playing basketball, but I **pretend** to have fun.
3. I know it is true because Mary told me. She is an **honest** person.
4. I always feel **nervous** when my brother drives. He's not a good driver.
5. I don't like to speak in front of the class. I feel **embarrassed**.
6. I have a great **joke** to tell you. It is very funny.
7. The news didn't **surprise** Jim. Someone told him about it earlier.
8. Use a hat to **protect** your head from the sun.

a. ________ (*adjective*) worried or afraid about what may happen

b. ________ (*verb*) to keep someone or something safe

c. ________ (*noun*) something that you say or do to make people laugh

d. ________ (*adjective*) not made or caused by people

e. ________ (*adjective*) shy or worried about what other people think of you

f. ________ (*adjective*) saying what is true; not stealing, lying, or cheating

g. ________ (*verb*) to try to make someone believe something that is not true

h. ________ (*verb*) to do something that someone does not expect

PREVIEW READING 1

You are going to read an article from a news magazine about the different reasons people laugh.

Preview the article. What four questions does it ask about laughter?

CD 2
Track 3 **Read the magazine article.**

What Is Laughter?

1 Laughter is **natural** for people. We start to laugh at about four months of age. We start to laugh even before we start to speak!

2 Laughter connects us with other people. We laugh more when we are with other people. Studies find that we are 30 times more likely to laugh with other people than alone. Laughter is also contagious[1]. When one person laughs, other people begin to laugh, too.

Laughter is natural for people.

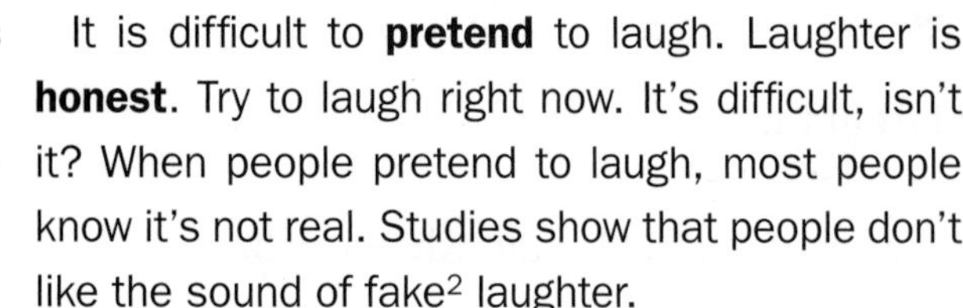

3 It is difficult to **pretend** to laugh. Laughter is **honest**. Try to laugh right now. It's difficult, isn't it? When people pretend to laugh, most people know it's not real. Studies show that people don't like the sound of fake[2] laughter.

When do people laugh?

4 Only 10 to 20 percent of laughter is about something funny. Most laughter is about being friendly with other people. Most laughter says, "I don't want to compete with you. I want to be friendly with you." This kind of laughter brings people together.

5 We often laugh when we feel **nervous**. In movies, there is often a joke at an exciting moment when everyone feels nervous. It is usually a small joke, but we laugh a lot. Our laughter helps us relax.

6 Sometimes we laugh because we think we are better than other people. When we laugh at another person, we are saying, "I am better than you." This kind of laughter makes others feel bad. Sometimes we laugh because we feel **embarrassed**.

What is funny?

7 Some things are funny because we don't expect them. When a **joke** begins, we already have an idea about the end. We think we know the end, but then the joke ends in a different way. The end of the joke **surprises** us. It makes us laugh.

8 Silly[3] things are sometimes funny. We laugh at jokes about people and their mistakes because we know something they don't know. We think we are better than they are.

Why doesn't everyone laugh at the same joke?

9 Not everyone has the same sense of humor[4]. Some people think a joke is funny, but other people don't think so. People have different ideas about what is funny.

10 Our idea of what is funny changes with time. For young children, the world is new. Many things surprise them, so they laugh a lot. Teenagers often worry about what others think of them. They laugh to **protect** themselves. Adults laugh at themselves and other people with similar problems. They laugh at things that give them stress. Our reasons for laughter change over time.

[1] **contagious:** passing from one person to another person very quickly
[2] **fake:** not real
[3] **silly:** not serious; stupid
[4] **sense of humor:** ability to feel or understand what is funny

MAIN IDEAS

Circle the best answer according to Reading 1.

1. Why do we laugh?
   a. because our parents teach us
   b. because it is natural to do
2. When do people laugh?
   a. mainly when they are alone
   b. mainly when they are with other people
3. What is funny?
   a. something we know very well
   b. something surprising or silly
4. Why doesn't everyone laugh at the same joke?
   a. Different things make different people laugh.
   b. Most people don't laugh in front of others.

DETAILS

Read the statements. Write *T* (true) or *F* (false).

____ 1. Laughter is always friendly.

____ 2. People sometimes laugh when they are surprised.

____ 3. People like it when others pretend to laugh.

____ 4. Young children often laugh because the world surprises them.

____ 5. A small joke in an exciting movie makes us relax.

____ 6. Young children laugh to protect themselves.

WHAT DO YOU THINK?

Ask and answer the questions with a partner. Then choose one question and write two to three sentences about it in your notebook.

1. Ask and answer the questions in the chart. Check (✓) your partner's answers. Add one more question to the chart.

Do you laugh . . .	Never	Sometimes	Often
1. . . . when you are nervous?	☒	☐	☒
2. . . . when you hear a joke?	☐	☐	☒
3. . . . when you hear other people laugh?	☐	☒	☐
4. . . . when you are embarrassed?	☒	☐	☐
5. . . . when something surprises you?	☐	☒	☐
6. . . . when my grand son dances?	☐	☐	☒

2. Who are you with when you laugh a lot? Where are you? What are you doing?
whith my son in love
at home of my daugther
at lunch

Reading Skill Identifying the topic sentence in a paragraph

The **topic sentence** explains the main idea of a paragraph. Other sentences in a paragraph support the topic sentence. Often, the topic sentence is the first sentence of a paragraph, but sometimes it is the second or third sentence. Finding the topic sentence helps you quickly understand what the paragraph is about.

Robert Provine studied people and laughter. **He discovered that people laugh when they want to be friendly.** He watched people in the city walking and shopping. He found that 80 to 90 percent of laughter came after sentences like *I know* or *I'll see you later.* People didn't laugh because someone said something funny. People laughed because they wanted to be friendly with each other.

A. Read the paragraphs. Underline the topic sentence in each paragraph and write *TS* next to it.

1. Many people say, "I just don't laugh very much. I can't change that." That's not true! People can learn to laugh. First, you need to see how small events can be funny. For example, you are carrying too many bags, and you drop one bag. Laugh at the situation. Second, you can learn to be funny and tell jokes. Watch funny TV shows and read jokes on the Internet. Give yourself more reasons to laugh. You can learn to bring laughter into your life.

2. Laughter happens at certain times in a conversation. People laugh more when they speak than when they listen. Pay attention to conversations around you. You will discover that the speaker in a conversation laughs more often. Also, laughter almost always comes at the end of a sentence or a thought. For example, a person might say, "He went to the wrong store! Ha! Ha! Ha!" The person does not say, "He went—Ha! Ha! Ha!—to the wrong store!"

B. Look at Reading 1 again. Underline the topic sentence in each paragraph and write *TS* next to it.

READING 2 | The Best Medicine Is Laughter

VOCABULARY

Tip for Success

Write new vocabulary in a small notebook. Write a definition for each word. Add to the vocabulary list every day.

Here are some words from Reading 2. Read the sentences. Then write each bold word next to the correct definition.

1. **Breathe** deeply. It helps you relax.
2. I read at a slow **rate**. I only read a few words per minute.
3. People **cry** when they are sad, but they also cry when they are very happy.
4. Laughter has a good **effect** on your body and your health.
5. Eating healthy food and getting exercise can **prevent** many illnesses.
6. I have a back problem. I feel **pain** in my back when I move.
7. I want more laughter in my life. I want to **increase** how much I laugh.
8. He has a **fear** of dogs because a dog bit him when he was young.

a. ______________ (*noun*) a change that happens because of something

b. ______________ (*verb*) to stop someone from doing something; to stop something from happening

c. ______________ (*noun*) the feeling that you have in your body when you are hurt or sick

d. ______________ (*noun*) the speed of something or how often something happens

e. ______________ (*verb*) to take in and let out air through your nose and mouth

f. ______________ (*verb*) to cause the amount, level, or number of something to go up

g. ______________ (*noun*) the feeling that you have when you think that something bad might happen

h. ______________ (*verb*) to have water falling from your eyes because you are unhappy or hurt

PREVIEW READING 2

You are going to read an article from the website for International Laughter Clubs.

Preview the reading. Check (✓) your answer.

What do you think people do at the International Laughter Club?

☐ 1. practice laughing

☐ 2. learn to stop laughing so much

CD 2 Track 4

Read the article.

The Best Medicine Is Laughter

Reasons to Laugh

1 Laughter is good exercise. It makes you **breathe** quickly. Laughter makes your heart **rate** go up, and it can turn your face red. Laughter can even make you **cry**! Ten to fifteen minutes of laughing burns 50 calories[1]. It exercises your whole body.

2 Laughter has a positive **effect** on your health. It reduces high blood pressure[2] and can **prevent** some illnesses. Also, laughter reduces **pain**, and it **increases** your ability to fight other illnesses. Laughter is good for you.

3 Laughter helps your brain. When you laugh often, you can remember information better. It improves your ability to think.

4 Laughter also changes how you feel. We often keep bad feelings inside. Feelings such as anger, sadness, and **fear** can cause stress. When we laugh, we let go of stress and bad feelings.

International Laughter Clubs

5 At International Laughter Clubs, we learn to laugh well. Our teachers show us how to laugh together. We learn to laugh with our whole body. We learn to breathe deeply when we laugh.

6 We practice laughter. In one laughter exercise, we stand in a circle. We put our hands on our face, chest, or stomach. Then we make "ha ha" or "hee hee" sounds until we laugh. Everyone in the circle starts laughing because laughter is so contagious!

7 We have 4,000 laughter clubs in 50 different countries all around the world. Our clubs are open to everyone. We have clubs in hospitals, schools, colleges, businesses, and nursing homes[3]. Laughter is a gift. Use it, and you can be healthy and happy.

Laughter uses many parts of your body.

an International Laughter Club

[1] **calorie:** a unit for measuring the energy value of food

[2] **blood pressure:** the rate at which your blood pushes through your body

[3] **nursing home:** a place where very old people live to get the special care they need

MAIN IDEAS

Write the correct paragraph number (1–7) next to each main idea.

___ a. There are International Laughter Clubs in many different countries and places.

___ b. Laughter has a positive effect on your feelings.

___ c. Laughter improves your health.

___ d. People at the clubs practice laughing.

___ e. Laughter helps you think better.

___ f. Laughter exercises your body.

___ g. International Laughter Clubs help people improve their laughter.

DETAILS

Read the statements. Write *T* (true) or *F* (false).

___ 1. Laughter increases blood pressure.

___ 2. When we laugh, we feel less pain.

___ 3. We feel less stress when we laugh.

___ 4. Laughter causes you to forget information.

___ 5. Laughter can prevent illnesses.

___ 6. Laughter clubs are not for old people.

WHAT DO YOU THINK?

A. Complete the activities in a group.

1. What happens to you when you laugh for a long time? How do you feel after you laugh? Use ideas from the box or your own ideas.

breathe deeply	cry	heart rate increases
breathe quickly	face turns red	stomach hurts

2. Read paragraph 6 of Reading 2 again (page 109). With your group, try the exercise in paragraph 6. Then discuss the questions.
   a. Did everyone laugh?
   b. How did you feel after the exercise?
   c. Do you think an exercise like this can really help people? Why or why not?

B. Think about both Reading 1 and Reading 2 as you discuss the questions.

1. How can you get more laughter into your life?
2. Is it important for a person to have a sense of humor? Why or why not?

Vocabulary Skill Using the dictionary

When you see a word you don't know in a text, it helps to **identify the part of speech** of the word. *Nouns*, *verbs*, *adjectives*, and *adverbs* are examples of parts of speech. Knowing the part of speech helps you better understand the meaning and use of the word. If you aren't sure, you can find the part of speech for the vocabulary words in this book on the last page of each unit (in *Track Your Success*). You can also find the part of speech in a dictionary.

laugh[1] /læf/ *verb* (**laughs, laugh·ing, laughed**) to make sounds to show that you are happy or that you think something is funny: *His jokes always make me laugh.*	**laugh**[2] /læf/ *noun* [*count*] the sound you make when you are happy or when you think something is funny: *My brother has a loud laugh.* • *She told us a joke and we all* ***had a good laugh*** (= laughed a lot).

You can see that there are two entries for *laugh*. One entry is a noun, and one is a verb. Some dictionaries use an abbreviation (a short form) to identify the part of speech.

n. = noun	adj. = adjective
v. = verb	adv. = adverb

When you know the part of speech, you can use the word correctly in a sentence.

✓ She laughs at my jokes.
✗ She laughter at my jokes.

A. **Read each sentence in the chart below. Then write the part of speech of the underlined word. Then check your answers in a dictionary.**

	Part of Speech
1. I feel embarrassed when I meet new people.	
2. Laughter stops anger.	
3. Laughter protects you from some illnesses.	
4. We breathe differently when we laugh.	
5. Laughter has many healthy effects on the body.	
6. I laugh a lot with my friends.	
7. The whole group laughs together in a laughing exercise.	
8. Laughter makes you breathe quickly.	

Tip for Success

Example sentences in the dictionary show us how words are used in sentences.

B. **The underlined words are the incorrect part of speech. Rewrite each sentence using the correct part of speech. Use your dictionary to help you.**

1. They are laughing because they are embarrassment.

____

2. I want to introduction you to my friend John.

____

3. Laughter is a gift from natural.

____

4. Try to breath deeply.

____

5. Laughter exercises can prevention some illnesses.

____

6. Her angry goes away when she laughs.

____

WRITING

Grammar Sentences with *when*

You can combine two sentences with *when*. *When* introduces a situation or state, and it means that anytime that situation or state happens, something else happens.

- There is a comma if the sentence begins with *when*. There is no comma if *when* is in the middle of the sentence.
- When the subject in both sentences is the same, use a pronoun in the second part of the sentence.

They are nervous. → They laugh.	Bob laughs. → He feels less stress.
When they are nervous, they laugh.	**When** Bob laughs, he feels less stress.
They laugh **when** they are nervous.	Bob feels less stress **when** he laughs.

A. Write two sentences with *when*. Remember that *when* introduces the situation or state that causes another situation or state.

1. I go out with my friends. → I laugh a lot.
   a. When I go out with my friends, I laugh a lot.
   b. I laugh a lot when I go out with my friends.
2. You laugh. → Your blood pressure goes down.
   a. ______
   b. ______
3. He sees something funny. → He laughs.
   a. ______
   b. ______
4. You laugh. → You use calories.
   a. ______
   b. ______

5. We hear a good joke. → We laugh.

a. ______________________________

b. ______________________________

6. She is nervous. → She laughs.

a. ______________________________

b. ______________________________

B. Complete each sentence with your own idea. Then read your sentences to a partner.

1. I laugh a lot when ______________________________.
2. I never laugh when ______________________________.
3. When I see someone fall, ______________________________.
4. When I am in class, ______________________________.
5. When I am nervous, ______________________________.
6. When I laugh, ______________________________.
7. When I am with my family, ______________________________.

Writing Skill | Writing a topic sentence

A good **topic sentence** is the first step in building a great paragraph. The topic sentence explains the main idea of the paragraph. It tells what the paragraph is about.

> **There are different kinds of laughter.** Some laughter is short and light. It comes from the throat. Other laughter comes from the stomach. This laughter is deep and loud. In addition, each person's laughter is different. No two laughs are exactly the same.

Writing a good topic sentence will help you better organize your writing and will make your writing clearer to readers.

A. **Match each topic sentence with the correct paragraph. Then write the topic sentence on the line.**

a. ~~When Bob is nervous, he laughs.~~
b. Mark relaxes when he laughs.
c. Paul laughs when he hears something funny.
d. Sam laughs to be friendly.

1. When Bob is nervous, he laughs.

For example, he laughs when he gets in trouble. He also laughs when he speaks in front of the class. In new situations, he makes jokes. Generally, my friend laughs when he is nervous.

2. ______________________________

For example, he laughs when he meets new people. He also laughs when he is with good friends. At parties, he always laughs. It's clear that he laughs to make people feel good.

3. ______________________________

When he laughs, his blood pressure goes down, and his bad feelings go away. He lets go of stress when he laughs. Laughter helps him stop feeling worried about things.

4. ______________________________

He laughs when he watches funny TV shows. When his friends tell jokes, he laughs. He also laughs when he reads funny books. He has a great sense of humor and likes to laugh at comedy and at life.

B. **Read the paragraph. Then write a topic sentence.**

____

He goes there once a month and does laughing exercises in his group. After he practices laughing for two hours, he feels great. Lee laughs a lot at the laughing club.

Unit Assignment | Write a paragraph about what makes someone laugh

In this assignment, you are going to write a paragraph explaining what makes you or someone you know laugh. As you prepare your paragraph, think about the Unit Question, "What makes you laugh?" and refer to the Self-Assessment checklist on page 118.

For alternative unit assignments, see the *Q: Skills for Success Teacher's Handbook.*

Plan and Write

A. BRAINSTORM Think of situations that make you or someone you know laugh. Complete the chart with three situations for each type of laughter. Use vocabulary from the unit when you can.

Type of Laughter	Situations That Make You or Someone You Know Laugh
Nervous or embarrassed	1. 2. 3.
Something is funny	1. 2. 3.
Want to be friendly	1. 2. 3.

B. PLAN Complete the activities to organize your paragraph.

1. Write a topic sentence for your paragraph. Choose and complete one of the sentence frames below, or write your own. Use information from Activity A to help you choose a topic.

   a. (I laugh / My ________________ laughs) when something makes (me / him / her) nervous or embarrassed.

   b. (I laugh / My ________________ laughs) when something is funny.

   c. (I laugh / My ________________ laughs) when (I want / he wants / she wants) to be friendly.

   d. (I laugh / My ________________ laughs) when ________________.

Step 2 asks you to **outline** your paragraph. **Outlining** helps you to see the different parts of your writing. It is a very good way to organize your ideas.

2. Complete the outline. Use the information from your chart in Activity A, your topic sentence in Activity B1, and the example paragraphs on page 115, Activity A to help you.

> 1. Topic Sentence
>
> ____
>
> ____
>
> 2. Supporting Sentences
>
> ____
>
> ____
>
> ____
>
> 3. Concluding Sentence
>
> ____

C. WRITE Write your paragraph in your notebook. Look at the Self-Assessment checklist on page 118 to guide your writing.

REVISE AND EDIT

A. PEER REVIEW Read a partner's paragraph. Answer the questions and discuss them with your partner.

1. Is there a topic sentence? Write *TS* next to the topic sentence.
2. Are there three supporting sentences? Write *SS* next to each supporting sentence.
3. Is there a concluding sentence? Write *CS* next to the concluding sentence.
4. Is there something you don't understand? Write a question mark (?) in the margin.

B. REWRITE Review the answers to the questions in Activity A. You may want to revise and rewrite your paragraph.

C. **EDIT** **Complete the Self-Assessment checklist as you prepare to write the final draft of your paragraph. Be prepared to hand in your work or discuss it in class.**

SELF-ASSESSMENT		
Yes	No	
☐	☐	Is the first line of the paragraph indented?
☐	☐	Does every sentence begin with a capital letter?
☐	☐	Does every sentence have final punctuation?
☐	☐	Does every sentence have a subject and a verb?
☐	☐	Does every subject and verb agree?
☐	☐	Is the spelling correct? Check a dictionary if you are not sure.
☐	☐	Does the paragraph have vocabulary words from the unit?
☐	☐	Are sentences with *when* correct?
☐	☐	Does the paragraph have a good topic sentence?

Track Your Success

Circle the words you learned in this unit.

Nouns	Verbs	Adjectives
effect 🔑	breathe 🔑	embarrassed 🔑
fear 🔑	cry 🔑	honest 🔑
joke 🔑	increase 🔑	natural 🔑
pain 🔑	pretend 🔑	nervous 🔑
rate 🔑	prevent 🔑	
	protect 🔑	
	surprise 🔑	

🔑 Oxford 2000 keywords

AWL Academic Word List

Check (✓) the skills you learned. If you need more work on a skill, refer to the page(s) in parentheses.

READING	○	I can identify the topic sentence in a paragraph. (p. 106)
VOCABULARY	○	I can identify parts of speech in the dictionary. (p. 111)
GRAMMAR	○	I can recognize and use sentences with *when*. (p. 113)
WRITING	○	I can write a topic sentence. (p. 114)
LEARNING OUTCOME	○	I can explain what makes me or someone I know laugh.

UNIT 7

Music

READING • identifying supporting sentences and details
VOCABULARY • the prefix *un-*
GRAMMAR • prepositions of location
WRITING • writing supporting sentences and details

LEARNING OUTCOME

Identify what type of music you like, where you listen to it, and how it makes you feel.

Unit QUESTION

How does music make you feel?

PREVIEW THE UNIT

A **Discuss these questions with your classmates.**

Do you have a favorite kind of music?

Do you like to go to stores or restaurants that play music?

Look at the photo. What is the boy doing?

B **Discuss the Unit Question above with your classmates.**

Listen to *The Q Classroom*, Track 5 on CD 2, to hear other answers.

C **Work in a group. Write three adjectives to describe each type of music or to describe how each type of music makes you feel.**

1 popular music

____

____

2 classical music

____

____

3 jazz music

____

____

4 hip-hop music

____

____

D **Check (✓) the places where you often hear music. Then discuss the questions with your group.**

☐ bank	☐ train station	☐ elevator
☐ library	☐ clothing store	☐ supermarket
☐ restaurant	☐ dentist's office	☐ business office
☐ coffee shop	☐ gym	☐ hospital

1. What kind of music do you hear in the places you checked?
2. Do you like the music in these places? Why or why not?
3. In a place you didn't check, why do you think there is no music there?

READING 1 | Music and Shopping

VOCABULARY

Here are some words from Reading 1. Read the sentences. Then write each bold word next to the correct definition.

Tip for Success
Remember to pay attention to the part of speech of each vocabulary word in the list. This helps you use the word correctly.

1. There was one **customer** in the jewelry store. He didn't buy anything.
2. Fast and loud music is **exciting**.
3. **According to** my friend, this restaurant is really good.
4. Please turn down the **volume**. The music is too loud.
5. I don't **notice** the music when I am at the dentist.
6. That song sounds **familiar**. I remember it from somewhere.
7. Loud music doesn't **fit** a bank. The music needs to be quiet.
8. **Serious** music is boring. I like fun music.

a. ________________ (*noun*) a person who buys things from a store or other business

b. ________________ (*verb*) to be the right size, shape, or type for someone or something

c. ________________ (*adjective*) causing you to have strong feelings of happiness and interest

d. ________________ (*noun*) the amount of sound that something makes

e. ________________ (*adjective*) not funny; not joking or playing

f. ________________ (*verb*) to see or pay attention to someone or something

g. ________________ (*adjective*) that you know well

h. ________________ (*phrase*) as someone or something says

PREVIEW READING 1

This is an excerpt from a textbook. It explains the use of music in stores.

How do you think loud music changes the way people shop? Check (✓) your idea.

Loud music in stores makes people buy ________________.

- ☐ more
- ☐ less
- ☐ the same amount

CD 2 Track 6 **Read the excerpt.**

Music and Shopping

1 Stores play music to change the way customers feel. Bookstores play classical music. It makes the **customers** feel intelligent. Clothing stores for teenagers play popular music. It is **exciting** and makes the customers feel happy. But music does more than change the way customers feel. It can change the way a person shops. What do store managers and owners think about when they choose music?

Music Volume

2 **According to** studies, the **volume** of music changes how people shop. Customers shop quickly when store music is very loud. They hurry through the store, but they buy just as much. The rate of sales[1] per minute in loud stores is high. When music is quiet, customers shop slowly. Customers take time to look at the products and talk with the salespeople. Quiet music is good for products that take time and information to buy. Music volume changes how much time customers take to shop.

Music Tempo[2]

3 According to studies, slow music makes people slow down. In restaurants with slow music, customers spend more time eating. Slow music also slows down customers in supermarkets. Customers **notice** more products as they walk through the store. With slow music in supermarkets, sales go up by 38 percent. Slow music makes customers buy more.

Kind of Music

4 The kind of music a store plays can change a customer's sense of time. According to studies, **familiar** music gives shoppers a good idea of time. People know the

[1] **sales:** the number of things a business sells

[2] **tempo:** the speed of a piece of music

beginning, middle, and end of a familiar song. When customers hear music that is *not* familiar, they don't notice the time. When they don't notice the time, they spend more time shopping and buy more.

5 The kind of music a store plays can have an effect on the shopper's thoughts and feelings. People remember past experiences and feelings when they hear familiar music. Many stores play old, happy music so customers feel good. When customers hear *new* music, they forget about the world outside of the store. Some stores use new music so their customers relax while they shop. There are good reasons to choose different kinds of music.

The Music Matches the Product

6 Stores choose music that **fits** their products. A popular sports store plays popular music that is fast and exciting. It sells products to young people. Young people usually have a lot of energy[3]. A bookstore plays quiet classical music and jazz. It gives the store a **serious** and intelligent feeling. The music in a store matches the store and its products.

7 Store music changes the way people shop. It can make a person shop quickly or slowly. It can change the way shoppers feel and the way they think about the store and its products.

[3] **energy:** the ability to be active without getting tired

MAIN IDEAS

Circle the answer that best completes each statement according to Reading 1.

1. The kind of music a store plays can change the way people ______.
a. walk b. talk c. shop

2. Customers spend ______ time shopping when they hear slow music.
a. less b. the same amount of c. more

3. Customers don't notice the time when a store plays ______.
a. music they don't know b. fast and loud music c. familiar music

4. Stores play music that fits their ______.
a. volume b. products c. sales

DETAILS

Circle the answer that best completes each statement.

1. With loud music, the rate of sales per minute goes up because ______.
   a. people like loud music
   b. people make fast decisions
2. Quiet music is probably good for selling ______.
   a. foreign cars
   b. clothes
3. With slow music, sales go up because ______.
   a. people spend more time shopping
   b. people like slow music
4. People think of ______ when they hear familiar music.
   a. past experiences
   b. good prices
5. Some sports stores play popular fast music because ______.
   a. it makes people move quickly
   b. it fits the store and its products

WHAT DO YOU THINK?

Discuss the questions in a group. Then choose one question and write two to three sentences about it in your notebook.

1. Think about a store or restaurant you like. What kind of music does it play? Do you like the music? Tell your partner.
2. Make a music plan for a business that you want to own.
   - What kind of business is it?
   - What does it sell?
   - Who are the customers?
   - What kind of music does it play?

Reading Skill Identifying supporting sentences and details 

When you read a paragraph, it's important to understand how the writer supports the main idea. Good readers learn to look for the **supporting sentences** and **details**.

Supporting sentences

After you find the main idea or topic sentence in a paragraph, look for the supporting sentences. These sentences explain more about the topic sentence. The bold sentences below support the idea expressed in the topic sentence.

> Stores play music to change the way customers feel. **Bookstores play classical music.** It makes the customers feel intelligent. **Clothing stores for teenagers play popular music.** It is exciting and makes the customers feel happy.

Details

One or more details often follow a supporting sentence. The details give additional information about the supporting sentence. Each detail in the example paragraph explains why the store plays that music.

> Stores play music to change the way customers feel. Bookstores play classical music. **It makes the customers feel intelligent.** Clothing stores for teenagers play popular music. **It is exciting and makes the customers feel happy.**

When you read, underline the topic sentence of a paragraph and put a check (✓) next to each supporting sentence. That way you can see how the paragraph is organized.

A. Read Paragraphs 4 and 5 of Reading 1 again. Underline the topic sentence and put a check (✓) next to the two supporting sentences in each paragraph. Then compare your work with a partner.

Tip Critical Thinking

In Activities A and B, you have to **differentiate** between the topic sentence and the support sentences in a paragraph. **Differentiate** means to tell the difference between the two things. It can help you understand ideas better.

B. Read the paragraphs from Reading 1. Then write the type of sentence for each sentence.

TS = topic sentence
SS = supporting sentence
D = detail

Paragraph 2	
1. According to studies, the volume of music changes how people shop.	
2. Customers shop quickly when store music is very loud.	
3. They hurry through the store, but they buy just as much.	
4. The rate of sales per minute in loud stores is high.	
5. When music is quiet, customers shop slowly.	
6. Customers take time to look at the products and talk with the salespeople.	
7. Quiet music is good for products that take time and information to buy.	
Paragraph 3	
8. According to studies, slow music makes people slow down.	
9. In restaurants with slow music, customers spend more time eating.	
10. Slow music also slows down customers in supermarkets.	
11. Customers notice more products as they walk through the store.	
12. With slow music in supermarkets, sales go up by 38 percent.	

READING 2 | Music and the Movies

VOCABULARY

Here are some words from Reading 2. Read their definitions. Then complete each sentence.

action (*noun*) exciting things that happen
character (*noun*) a person in a book, play, television show, or movie
composer (*noun*) a person who writes music
director (*noun*) a person in charge of a movie who tells the actors what to do
instrument (*noun*) a thing that you use for playing music
level (*noun*) the amount, size, or number of something
perfectly (*adverb*) in a way that is so good that it cannot be better
scene (*noun*) part of a play or movie
tense (*adjective*) making people feel worried and not relaxed

1. He was a great speaker. I understood all his ideas ________________.
2. The little girl, Annie, is the most important ________________ in the movie.
3. The guitar is probably the most popular ________________ in the world.
4. The best part of the movie is the ________________ when the boy sees the cat again.
5. The movie was a little boring at first, but there was plenty of ________________ when Jackie Chan came on.
6. The ________________ of the sound in that movie was too high. It hurt my ears.
7. Driving in bad weather can be a(n) ________________ situation.
8. My favorite ________________ is Mozart.
9. The ________________ gives actors instructions.

PREVIEW READING 2

This is an article on an entertainment website. It explains how movies use music to tell their stories.

How much music do you think you hear during an average movie? Check (✓) your idea.

☐ 15 minutes ☐ 30 minutes ☐ 50 minutes

CD 2 Track 7 **Read the article.**

Music and the Movies

1 Most movies have between 40 and 75 minutes of music, but we don't usually notice the music. Why not? Because the music and the **action** in the movie fit **perfectly**.

2 The movie **director** and the music **composer** work together to make the music and the movie match. First, the director makes the movie. Then the director and the composer talk about every **scene** and **character**. The composer writes or chooses music for each scene in the movie. When the music doesn't fit the scene perfectly, the director cuts or changes parts of the scene. This way, the music matches the action in the movie perfectly.

string instruments

3 Music does many things for movies. First of all, it tells you the time and place of the movie. For example, a movie in downtown Hong Kong might play popular Chinese music. A movie in the U.S. in the 1960s might play rock 'n' roll. The music tells you where and when the movie takes place.

4 The music also tells you the **level** of action in a scene. A scene with lots of action has fast and loud music. A slow scene has slow and gentle[1] music. The music matches the speed of the scene.

5 The composer carefully chooses the musical **instruments** in order to let us know how people feel in each scene. Usually, sad scenes use string instruments. Scenes about war use brass instruments. Scenes that are **tense** use percussion instruments.

percussion instruments

6 Sometimes the music also explains how the characters in the movie grow and change. In some movies,

[1] **gentle:** not strong or unpleasant

brass instruments

the composer writes a piece of music for the main characters in the movie. We hear that piece of music every time the character is in a scene. This music can change as the character changes. For example, in the movie *Star Wars*, the music for the character of Luke Skywalker changes as he grows up. When Luke is a young boy, his music uses string instruments. When Luke grows up into a strong man, his music is played with a large number of instruments including a lot of brass instruments.

7 Music is an important part of the movie experience. The next time you go to the movies, be sure to notice the music. Think about the meaning of the music, and remember all the work that went into choosing and making it.

Main Ideas

Write *TS* next to topic sentences and *SS* next to supporting sentences.

Paragraph 2

____ a. The movie director and the music composer work together to make the music and the movie match.

____ b. When the music doesn't fit the scene perfectly, the director cuts or changes parts of the scene.

Paragraph 3

____ a. First of all, it tells you the time and place of the movie.

____ b. A movie in the U.S. in the 1960s might play rock 'n' roll.

Paragraph 4

____ a. The music also tells you the level of action in a scene.

____ b. A slow scene has slow and gentle music.

Paragraph 5

____ a. The composer carefully chooses the musical instruments in order to let us know how people feel in each scene.

____ b. Scenes about war use brass instruments.

Details

A. Read the statements. Write *T* (true) or *F* (false).

____ 1. The director and the composer work together.

____ 2. Action scenes go well with gentle music.

____ 3. String instruments are used for sad scenes.

____ 4. Brass instruments fit war scenes.

____ 5. Percussion instruments are good for tense scenes.

____ 6. The music for a main character is the same during the whole movie.

B. Read these steps for making the music for a movie. Order the steps (1–4).

____ a. The director and composer talk about every scene and character.

____ b. The director cuts parts of the movie to fit the music.

____ c. The director makes the movie.

____ d. The composer writes or chooses the music for the movie.

What Do You Think?

A. Discuss the questions in a group.

1. Look at the photos. What kind of music and what instruments best fit each movie scene?

1

2

3

2. Think of a movie with music that you like. Why do you like the music?

B. **Think about both Reading 1 and Reading 2 as you discuss the questions.**

1. In Reading 1, you read that music has an effect on how you shop. Does music have an effect on the type of movies you like? Why or why not?
2. What kind of shopping or movie do you think fits with very loud and fast music? Explain your answer.

Vocabulary Skill The prefix *un-* web

A **prefix** is a letter or group of letters at the beginning of a word. A prefix changes the meaning of a word. You can build your vocabulary by using prefixes. The prefix *un-* means *not*. It gives an adjective the opposite meaning.

familiar → **un**familiar (not familiar)

Only some adjectives can use the prefix *un-*:

✓ unlucky
✗ unfast

If you are unsure, check a dictionary before adding *un-* to an adjective.

A. **Only some of these words can use *un-*. Look in the dictionary and find the seven words that use *un-*. Write the word with its prefix on the line. Write *not* + word for the other three.**

1. bored	not bored	6. natural ______
2. friendly	unfriendly	7. quiet ______
3. happy	______	8. popular ______
4. important	______	9. similar ______
5. intelligent	______	10. usual ______

B. **Write five sentences. Use adjectives from Activity A. Then read your sentences aloud to a partner.**

1. ______
2. ______
3. ______
4. ______
5. ______

WRITING

Grammar Prepositions of location

The prepositions *on*, *in*, and *at* are **prepositions of location**. They describe where something or someone is.

- Use *in* with large areas such as continents and countries.

  in Europe **in** China **in** Australia

- Use *in* with the meaning of inside.

  in a store **in** a box **in** a car

- Use *at* with these places.

  at work **at** home **at** school

- Use *at* when talking about activities at places or businesses with names.

  We went shopping **at** the new mall.
  Let's have lunch **at** Frisco's Restaurant.

- Use *on* with roads.

  on the street **on** the highway **on** Main Street

- Use *on* with most large forms of transportation.

  on a plane **on** a ship **on** a train **on** a bus

A. Complete each sentence with the preposition *in*, *at*, or *on*.

1. Some people like to listen to music _______ work.
2. She listens to her MP3 player _______ the bus.
3. Many teachers do not let children listen to music _______ school.
4. Some towns play music _______ the street.
5. Sandra is taking a two-week vacation _______ Africa.
6. Teenagers like to listen to music _______ the car.
7. I listen to music all the time _______ home.
8. We went to hear that band _______ the Nashville Music Hall.

B. **Complete each sentence with a place where you do or don't like to listen to music. Discuss your answers with a partner.**

1. I like to listen to music ___on the train___.
2. I like to listen to music ________________.
3. I like to listen to music ________________.
4. I don't like to listen to music ________________.
5. I don't like to listen to music ________________.

Writing Skill | Writing supporting sentences and details

Supporting sentences explain the topic sentence in more detail. When you write an academic paper (for school), it is important to include two or three supporting sentences. It is also important to include **details**. Details give more information about each supporting sentence. Details include *examples, reasons, facts, dates,* and *numbers*. The underlined sentences in the example are supporting sentences. The check marks (✓) are at the beginning of each detail. It is often good to write a list of every detail you can think of and then choose only the best ones.

> Popular songs work well in television and radio advertisements. <u>Popular music is familiar and fun.</u> ✓ It makes the product seem familiar and fun. <u>People often sing along with popular songs.</u> ✓ People remember the advertisement because they sing along with the music. Popular songs make advertisements more familiar, memorable, and fun.

A. **Read the paragraph and underline the three supporting sentences. Then put a check (✓) at the beginning of each detail.**

I like to listen to music in different places. I like to listen to classical music at work. It makes me feel intelligent and serious. I like to listen to fast and loud music in the car. It makes me feel energetic and happy. I like to listen to string music in bed. It makes me feel quiet and relaxed. I like to hear music in many different places.

B. **Read each topic sentence. Then choose the best supporting sentence from the box below for the topic sentence. Write them on the lines. Do not write details yet.**

1. Music changes the way people feel.

   Supporting sentence: ______________________

   Detail: ______________________

   Supporting sentence: ______________________

   Detail: ______________________

2. Music is natural for people.

   Supporting sentence: ______________________

   Detail: ______________________

   Supporting sentence: ______________________

   Detail: ______________________

Supporting Sentences

a. Music with a quick tempo makes people feel happy.
b. Babies like the sound of music.
c. People all over the world have music.
d. Slow music makes people feel sad.

C. **Choose the best detail from the box for each supporting sentence in Activity B. Write the details on the lines in Activity B.**

Details

a. Mothers all over the world sing to their babies.
b. Songs in movies are not usually fast when someone dies.
c. It's fun to listen to dance music when shopping for clothes.
d. Many countries have their own string instrument.

Unit Assignment | Write a paragraph about how music makes you feel

In this assignment, you are going to write a paragraph about music, the places you listen to it and how it makes you feel. As you prepare your paragraph, think about the Unit Question, "How does music make you feel?" and refer to the Self-Assessment checklist on page 138.

For alternative unit assignments, see the *Q: Skills for Success Teacher's Handbook*.

PLAN AND WRITE

Tip for Success

Introduce the topic early in your paragraph and only give information that supports the topic.

A. BRAINSTORM Think of places where you like to hear music. What type of music is it, and how does it make you feel? Complete the chart and then tell a partner.

Place: ______________________________

Music: ______________________________

Feeling: ______________________________

B. PLAN Choose three places to write about and complete the sentences. Use vocabulary words from the unit when you can.

web Your Writing Process

Talking about your ideas with your classmates can help you plan your writing. See Stage 1B, *Talking About Your Ideas*, in *Q Online Practice*.

Topic sentence: Music in different places gives me different feelings.

Supporting sentence: I like to listen to ______________ music

(in / at / on) ______________________________.

Detail: It makes me feel ______________________________.

Supporting sentence: ______________________________.

Detail: ______________________________.

Supporting sentence: ______________________________.

Detail: ______________________________.

Concluding sentence: ______________________________.

C. WRITE Write your paragraph in your notebook. Look at the Self-Assessment checklist on page 138 to guide your writing.

Revise and Edit

A. **PEER REVIEW** **Read a partner's paragraph. Answer the questions and discuss them with your partner.**

1. Is there a topic sentence? Write *TS* next to the topic sentence.
2. Are there three supporting sentences? Write *SS* next to each supporting sentence.
3. Are there details to support the supporting sentences?
4. Is there a concluding sentence? Write *CS* next to the concluding sentence.
5. Is there something you don't understand? Write a question mark (?) in the margin.

B. **REWRITE** **Review the answers to the questions in Activity A. You may want to revise and rewrite your paragraph.**

C. **EDIT** **Complete the Self-Assessment checklist as you prepare to write the final draft of your paragraph. Be prepared to hand in your work or discuss it in class.**

SELF-ASSESSMENT		
Yes	No	
☐	☐	Is the first line of the paragraph indented?
☐	☐	Does every sentence begin with a capital letter?
☐	☐	Does every sentence have final punctuation?
☐	☐	Does every sentence have a subject and a verb?
☐	☐	Does every subject and verb agree?
☐	☐	Is the spelling correct? Check a dictionary if you are not sure.
☐	☐	Does the paragraph have vocabulary words from the unit?
☐	☐	Are the prepositions of location correct?

Track Your Success

Circle the words you learned in this unit.

Nouns	Verbs	Adverb
action 🔑	fit 🔑	perfectly
character 🔑	notice 🔑	**Phrase**
composer	**Adjectives**	according to 🔑
customer 🔑	exciting 🔑	
director	familiar 🔑	
instrument 🔑	serious 🔑	
level 🔑	tense AWL	
scene		
volume 🔑 AWL		

🔑 Oxford 2000 keywords

AWL Academic Word List

Check (✓) the skills you learned. If you need more work on a skill, refer to the page(s) in parentheses.

READING	I can identify supporting sentences and details. (p. 127)
VOCABULARY	I can recognize and use the prefix ***un-***. (p. 133)
GRAMMAR	I can recognize and use prepositions of location. (p. 134)
WRITING	I can write supporting sentences and details. (p. 135)
LEARNING OUTCOME	I can identify what type of music I like, where I listen to it, and how it makes me feel.

UNIT 8

Honesty

READING • identifying pronoun referents
VOCABULARY • collocations
WRITING • writing concluding sentences
GRAMMAR • infinitives of purpose

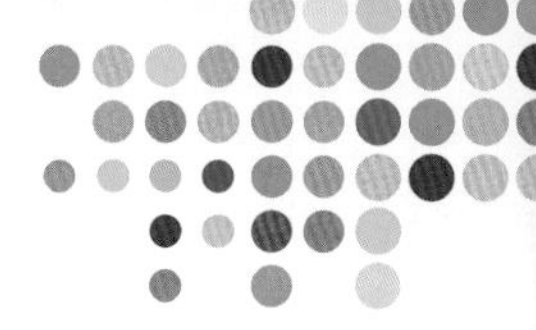

LEARNING OUTCOME

Write a paragraph that explains your opinion about whether or not it is OK to lie in an online forum.

Unit QUESTION

Is it ever OK to lie?

PREVIEW THE UNIT

A **Discuss these questions with your classmates.**

Do you think children lie more than adults?

What kinds of things do people lie about?

Look at the photo. Where is the woman?
What is she doing?

B **Discuss the Unit Question above with your classmates.**

Listen to *The Q Classroom*, Track 8 on CD 2, to hear other answers.

C Complete the activities.

1. Read each situation. Imagine you are in the situation and choose your answer. Then discuss your choice with a partner.

> **Situation 1:** A classmate asks you to go to a movie. You don't want to. What do you say?
>
> Classmate: "Do you want to go to a movie tonight?"
>
> You: "I'm sorry. I can't go. I'm busy tonight." **OR** "No thanks. I don't really want to go."

> **Situation 2:** Your grandmother gives you a watch. You don't like it. What do you say?
>
> Grandmother: "Happy birthday! I got this for you."
>
> You: "Thank you. I really like it." **OR** "Thank you. It's not really my style, though."

2. Take turns role-playing each situation above with your partner. Can you think of another possible answer? You can use one of the answer choices or your own idea.

D Read each statement in the survey. Check (✓) *Agree* or *Disagree*. Then compare your answers in a group.

	Agree	Disagree
1. It's possible to tell the truth all of the time.		
2. People don't want to hear the truth.		
3. A good friend always tells the truth.		
4. Some lies are OK because they make people happy.		
5. All lies are wrong.		

READING

READING 1 | The Lies People Tell

VOCABULARY

Here are some words from Reading 1. Read their definitions. Then complete each sentence.

admit (*verb*) to say you did something wrong or that something bad is true
boss (*noun*) a person at a workplace who tells other people what to do
continue (*verb*) to go on or keep on; to not stop
control (*verb*) to make people or things do what you want
fire (*verb*) to tell someone to leave his or her job
furniture (*noun*) tables, chairs, beds
punishment (*noun*) something bad that happens to someone because he or she did something wrong
reputation (*noun*) what people say or think about someone or something
trouble (*noun*) a difficulty or problem

1. My grandparents have ________________ with their loud neighbors.
2. These chairs are really old. I need some new ________________.
3. Johnny, you were late. Your ________________ is to stay after school.
4. Samantha never listens and doesn't follow company rules. I think we need to ________________ her.
5. It is difficult to ________________ children. They have lots of energy when they are young.
6. I'm sorry. I ________________ that I made a mistake.
7. People say he is a very good worker and an honest person. He has an excellent ________________.
8. Please stop telling me what to do all the time! You're not my ________________!
9. Our neighbor often tells us to be quiet, but we ________________ to play loud music every night.

Preview Reading 1

This is a magazine article about the different kinds of lies people tell.

Preview the article. Check (✓) two topics you think you will read about.

Topics

- ☐ how to tell a lie
- ☐ the lies people often tell
- ☐ what to do when a person lies to you
- ☐ why people tell lies

CD 2 Track 9 **Read the article.**

The Lies People Tell

Most people don't **admit** it, but people often tell lies. These are nine lies people often tell.

Lie 1: "You look great!"

A woman asks her husband, "Does my hair look OK?" The husband doesn't like it, but he says something nice. He says, "You look great!" Why? He wants his wife to be happy. He doesn't want to hurt her feelings.

Lie 2: "I didn't do it!"

A boy breaks a cup. His mother asks, "Who broke the cup?" The boy says, "I didn't do it." Why? The boy did something wrong. He is afraid of the **punishment**. He tells a lie so he doesn't get in **trouble**.

Lie 3: "He came to work on time."

Lina works in an office. Another worker in her office, Pete, has trouble with his car. Pete often arrives late to work. The **boss** is not happy with him. The boss asks Lina, "Did Pete come to work on time today?" He didn't, but Lina says, "Yes." Why? She lies to protect him.

"I didn't do it."

Lie 4: "The cat went to a farm."

The family cat dies. "It went to a farm to play with other cats," say the parents. They don't say the cat died. Why not? They lie to protect their children from the truth. They think it will hurt too much.

Lie 5: "You won't get any gifts!"

A boy hits his little sister at his birthday party. The parents say, "Stop! You won't get your gifts if you hit her again!" This is not true. They plan to give their son his gifts even if he **continues** to behave badly[1]. Why do they tell a lie? They lie to **control** their son.

[1] **behave badly:** to do or say things in a way that is wrong

Lie 6: "The fish was three feet long!"

Joe is telling a story about his fishing trip. He says a fish he caught was three feet long, but it wasn't really very big. Why? He lies in order to tell a more interesting story.

Lie 7: "I can speak three languages."

Pamela tells her classmates, "I can speak three languages." She can really speak only two languages. Why does she lie? She wants to make a good impression[2] on her new classmates. Pamela wants them to think she is very intelligent.

Lie 8: "This special price is for today only."

A store ad says it has special prices on **furniture** for today only. The truth is that the price is the same every day. Why does the store lie? It lies in order to make more money.

People tell lies for different reasons.

Customers buy more furniture when they believe the prices are special for one day only.

Lie 9: "Her boss fired her from her last job!"

A man tells people at work that a new worker's boss fired her from her last job. This is not true. The man tells the lie to hurt the other worker's **reputation**.

[2] **make a good impression:** to make people think good things about you

MAIN IDEAS

Why do people lie? Check (✓) the seven reasons from the article.

☐ 1. They want to be famous.
☐ 2. They want to protect someone.
☐ 3. They don't want to hurt someone's feelings.
☐ 4. They want to make a person laugh.
☐ 5. They want to make a good impression.
☐ 6. They want to make more money.
☐ 7. They don't want to get in trouble.
☐ 8. They want to control a child.
☐ 9. They want to get a job.
☐ 10. They want to hurt someone's reputation.

DETAILS

In the Unit 4 Reading Skill on page 66, you learned that good readers make inferences. Circle the best inference for each lie from Reading 1.

1. "You look great!"
   a. The man cares about his wife.
   b. The man likes short hair.
2. "I didn't do it!"
   a. The child's parents punish the child when he does something wrong.
   b. The child breaks things often.
3. "The cat went to a farm."
   a. The family will get a new cat.
   b. The children loved the family cat.
4. "Her boss fired her from her last job!"
   a. The man doesn't like the new worker.
   b. The new worker changes jobs a lot.

WHAT DO YOU THINK?

A. Check *OK* or *Not OK* for each lie from Reading 1.

	OK	Not OK
1. "You look great!"	☐	☐
2. "I didn't do it!"	☐	☐
3. "He came to work on time."	☐	☐
4. "The cat went to a farm."	☐	☐
5. "You won't get any gifts."	☐	☐
6. "The fish was three feet long!"	☐	☐
7. "I can speak three languages."	☐	☐
8. "This special price is for today only."	☐	☐

B. Discuss the questions in a group. Then choose one question and write three to four sentences about it in your notebook.

1. What is one lie from the chart in Activity A that you feel is OK? Why do you think so?
2. What is one lie from the chart in Activity A that you feel is not OK? Why do you think so?

Reading Skill | Identifying pronoun referents 

Pronouns take the place of nouns and avoid repetition.

✓ Brian says **he** is coming here tomorrow. (subject pronoun)
✗ Brian says **Brian** is coming here tomorrow.

✓ Brian says to call **him** this evening. (object pronoun).
✗ Brian says to call **Brian** this evening.

Here are the subject and object pronouns.

Subject Pronouns	Object Pronouns
I	me
you	you
he	him
she	her
it	it
we	us
they	them

To understand a pronoun, you need to identify the noun it refers to. The noun a pronoun refers to is called its **referent**. Look for

- a noun that comes **before** the pronoun. (It may be in a different sentence.)
- a noun that **agrees with** the pronoun in gender and number (For example, *he* agrees with *brother, she* does not; *it* agrees with *book*, *they* does not.)

If there are two or more possibilities, use the context to help you decide.

My sisters like to ride in sports cars, but they don't enjoy driving **them**.

It does not make sense for *sisters* to be the object of the verb *drive*. In this sentence, *them* refers back to *cars*.

Look at these examples.

Alice didn't do her homework. She lied to her teacher.

The machine doesn't work. It doesn't turn on.

Jim is very popular. His classmates like him.

The girls said, "Look at us!"

A. **Read the sentences and look at the pronouns in bold. Circle the noun the pronoun refers to.**

1. People say **they** always tell the truth.
2. A small lie can grow big. **It** has a life of its own.
3. Children start to lie at age four or five. **They** lie to get out of trouble.
4. Janet Cooke lied about the schools she went to. **She** said she went to very famous schools.
5. Writer Stephen Glass lied in his stories. He lied to make **them** more interesting.

B. **Read the excerpts from Reading 1 and look at the pronouns in bold. Then circle the noun each pronoun refers to.**

1. A woman asks her husband, "Do you like my hair?" The husband doesn't like **it**, but **he** says, "You look great!" Why? He wants **her** to be happy.
   a. **it:** woman / hair / husband
   b. **he:** woman / hair / husband
   c. **her:** woman / hair / husband
2. Lina works in an office. Another worker in her office, Pete, often has trouble with his car. The boss is not happy with **him. He** asks Lina, "Did Pete come to work on time today?" Lina says, "Yes." Why? **She** wants to protect him.
   a. **him:** Lina / Pete / boss
   b. **He:** Lina / Pete / boss
   c. **She:** Lina / Pete / boss
3. The family cat dies. "**It** went to a farm to play with other cats," say the parents. Why? **They** want to protect their children from the truth. The parents think **it** will hurt too much.
   a. **It:** cat / parents / truth
   b. **They:** cat / parents / truth
   c. **it:** cat / parents / truth
4. A boy hits his little sister at his birthday party. The parents say, "Stop! **You** won't get your presents if you hit **her** again." This is not true. **They** plan to give him the presents, even if he continues to behave badly.
   a. **You:** boy / sister / parents
   b. **her:** boy / sister/ parents
   c. **They:** boy / sister / parents

READING 2 | Honesty and Parenting

VOCABULARY

Here are some words from Reading 2. Read the sentences. Then write each bold word next to the correct definition.

1. The **purpose** of this activity is to learn new words.
2. I don't agree with your **opinion**. You think it's OK to lie, but I don't.
3. You can **trust** him. He never lies.
4. I **respect** my father very much. I want to be like him.
5. Jill and Rob have a good **relationship**. They take care of each other.
6. Good piano players **practice** every day.
7. People **require** eight hours of sleep a night. With less than eight hours of sleep, people get sick more often.
8. I try to **avoid** dangerous situations. That's why I don't go out after 11:00 at night.

a. ________________ (*noun*) what you think about something

b. ________________ (*verb*) to think good things about someone or something

c. ________________ (*verb*) to need something

d. ________________ (*verb*) to try *not* to do something

e. ________________ (*verb*) to believe that someone or something is honest and good and will not hurt you in any way

f. ________________ (*verb*) to do something many times so that you will do it well

g. ________________ (*noun*) the reason for doing something

h. ________________ (*noun*) the way people or groups feel about each other

Internet chat rooms are a good place to practice writing in English. Many English language students do this. Don't worry about mistakes. People only want to know what you think.

PREVIEW READING 2

You are going to read postings in an Internet chat room. In this chat room, parents talk about some of the problems they have with their children.

Skim the posts. What is Marisa worried about? Check (✓) your answer.

☐ not teaching soccer to her son
☐ not telling the truth to her son
☐ not punishing her son

CD 2 Track 10 **Read the chat room posts.**

Marisa

Is it ever OK for a parent to lie to a child? My 10-year-old son plays soccer. He's not very good, but he loves it. Yesterday he played very badly. When he finished the game, he said, "Did I play well?" I said, "Yes! You're a great soccer player!" Did I do the right thing?

Bay212

Yes, you did the right thing. You told your son a white lie[1]. Your **purpose** was to make him feel good. Now he's ready to play soccer again.

Bernie

In my **opinion**, you should be honest. Your son wanted to know the truth. He knew he didn't play well. In time, he will learn not to believe you. He will not **trust** you. He will not **respect** you. Honesty is the first step to a good parent-child **relationship**.

Missy

You lied to make your son feel better, but you missed an opportunity to teach him a life lesson. People need to work hard for what they want. Maybe next time you can say, "No, you didn't play well today. Great soccer players **practice** a lot. Let's go practice." The truth will make him strong and a good soccer player.

[1] **white lie:** a small lie that doesn't cause any harm

Pixie

What do you say to him when he plays a good game? Do you lie and say that he is a really great player so he believes you? Every lie **requires** five more lies.

HueyBoy

You worry too much. White lies are a necessary part of life. We need to lie to **avoid** hurting each other.

Linda

I don't think there is ever a good reason to lie to our children. I want my children to become honest adults. Children learn honesty from the examples they see. We need to be honest in order to teach honesty to our children.

Parviz

Children need honesty from their parents. Parents need to avoid lying, but they don't need to tell the whole truth. Next time, when your son asks, "Did I play well?" you can say, "What do you think?" Then your son can tell you what he thinks. That way, everything you say is true, and you avoid truth that hurts.

Main Ideas

Complete the chart. Check (✓) *Yes* or *No*.

Is it OK for Marisa to lie to her son about his soccer ability?	Yes	No
1. Bay212	☐	☐
2. Bernie	☐	☐
3. Missy	☐	☐
4. Pixie	☐	☐
5. HueyBoy	☐	☐
6. Linda	☐	☐
7. Parviz	☐	☐

Details

Look at Reading 2. Why is it OK for Marisa to lie? Why is it not OK? Write all the reasons in the chart.

Reasons It's OK to Lie	Reasons It's not OK to Lie
The son feels good about himself.	The son won't trust his mother.

What Do You Think?

A. Discuss the questions in a group.

1. Which person in Reading 2 do you agree with? Why?
2. Which person in Reading 2 do you disagree with? Why?

B. Think about both Reading 1 and Reading 2 as you discuss the questions.

1. What kinds of lies do parents sometimes tell their children?
2. Which lies are OK to tell children?

Vocabulary Skill | Collocations

Tip for Success

You can use a collocations dictionary to help you learn common collocations. You can also find collocation information in most dictionaries.

Collocations are words that often go together.

✓ make the bed
✗ do the bed

✓ do the dishes
✗ make the dishes

In the examples, *do the bed* and *make the dishes* are possible grammatically, but speakers do not use these words together. *Make the bed* and *do the dishes* are the collocations that we use. Learning common collocations will help you speak and write more naturally.

A. **Complete each collocation with a word or phrase from the box. These collocations are in Readings 1 and 2.**

someone's feelings	the right thing
the truth	a good impression
in trouble	a story
a lie	

1. tell ____________________
2. tell ____________________
3. tell ____________________
4. make ____________________
5. do ____________________
6. hurt ____________________
7. get ____________________

B. **Complete each sentence with a word or phrase from the box.**

truth	stories	the right thing
feelings	a good impression	trouble

1. He lies so often. I never know when he is telling me the ____________________.
2. I'm sorry I lied. I didn't want to hurt your ____________________.
3. Sometimes it's hard to do ____________________, but it's important to try.
4. Jim tells funny ____________________. I always laugh when he tells the one about the fish.
5. My parents know I lied. I really don't want to get in ____________________.
6. She answered the boss's questions very well. She made ____________________.

WRITING

Writing Skill | Writing concluding sentences 

A good **concluding sentence** closes the paragraph. Sometimes it tells the reader the main idea again. It does not add new information.

> Sometimes we lie for good reasons. We lie to make people feel good. We lie to make our stories more interesting. We lie to protect the people we love. **There are times when a lie is better than the truth.**

Note: Concluding sentences are important in long paragraphs. Sometimes, concluding sentences are not necessary in short paragraphs.

A. Complete each paragraph with the correct concluding sentence from the box.

a. Every day, adults lie to get out of trouble.
b. It's OK to lie if it makes someone feel good.
c. ~~Only truth can protect the people we love.~~
d. When a person avoids the truth, the person is lying.

1. Some lies seem OK, but they can hurt people in the end. We tell these small lies to make people happy. We tell these lies to protect the people we love. In the end, the truth always comes out. In the end, the people we love are hurt and unhappy.

   Only truth can protect the people we love.

2. Not only children lie to avoid punishment. Sometimes a fast driver lies to avoid a ticket from a police officer. Sometimes an employee lies to avoid trouble with the boss. Sometimes a friend lies to avoid making a friend angry.

   ____

3. A half-truth is a whole lie. For example, a wife wants to go on a family vacation. The husband asks, "Can we pay for this vacation?" The wife knows it is very expensive, but she says, "Yes, we can pay for it." She's thinking, "We can pay for it with credit cards." She doesn't explain the whole truth.

   ____

4. The only bad lies are the lies that hurt. Some people like to believe lies. They know the lies are not true, but they like to think they are. For example, someone says, "You make the best cup of coffee in the world." That probably isn't true, but it feels good to hear.

____

B. Write a concluding sentence for each paragraph. Then read your sentences to a partner.

1. Honesty is always the right way. Some people say that if the purpose of the lie is good, then the lie is OK. I don't think so. To have a good relationship, you need to respect and trust a person. It's not possible to trust and respect someone who lies.

____

____

2. I have a good friend named Alex. He is very honest with me. If I make a mistake, he tells me. I always know he will tell me the truth. I trust him.

____

____

3. It's important to be honest, but it's also important to be kind. Sometimes we have to make a decision between the two. In situations when the truth can hurt, I think it is better to say nothing.

____

____

Grammar Infinitives of purpose 

Infinitives to show purpose

As you learned in the Unit 2 Grammar on page 37, an infinitive is *to* + the base form of the verb, and it can come after the verbs *like*, *want*, and *need*. Another way you can use an infinitive is to give a purpose for someone's action. An **infinitive of purpose** explains why someone does something.

She lies to her child **to be** nice. (Why does she lie? Her purpose is to be nice.)
They lied **to make** more money. (Why did they lie? Their purpose was to make more money.)
They listen to music **to relax**. (Why do they listen to music? Their purpose is to relax.)
We laugh **to improve** our health. (Why do we laugh? Our purpose is to improve our health.)

In order + infinitive to show purpose

You can also use *in order* + an infinitive to show the purpose. The meaning is the same, but more formal. Use *in order* with negative infinitives.

She lies to her child **in order to be** nice.
She lies to her child **in order not to hurt** his feelings.

A. Look back at Reading 1. Underline all the examples of infinitives of purpose. Write the number of examples of each. Compare your results with a partner.

1. There are ___ examples of infinitives of purpose in Reading 1.
2. There are ___ examples of *in order* + infinitive in Reading 1.

B. Complete each sentence. Use an infinitive of purpose or *in order* + infinitive and a reason from the box.

make his friend feel good	make money	get out of trouble
protect his friend	hurt his friend	

Tip for Success

A quotation mark introduces the exact words a person said. Use a comma after the verbs *say*, *tell*, etc.

1. Dennis didn't do his homework. The teachers asked him for his homework. Dennis said, "I did it, but I left it at home on my desk."

   Dennis lied *to get out of trouble*.

2. A used car salesman said, "This car is in perfect condition." But the car has some serious problems.

   The salesman lied ____________________.

3. Jim is often in trouble in school. One day in class Jim broke a chair. The teacher asked the class, "Who broke this chair?" Jim's friend Gino said, "I did. I'm sorry. It was an accident."

   Gino lied ____________________.

4. John bought a ring for his mother. He showed the ring to his friend Sam. Sam thought it was ugly. Sam said, "The ring is beautiful. Your mother will love it."

   Sam lied ____________________.

5. Alex told Samir, "Nobody likes you." In fact, everyone likes Samir. Alex wants to be popular, too, but he isn't.

   Alex lied ____________________.

Unit Assignment | Write an opinion paragraph

In this assignment, you are going to write an opinion paragraph about lying online. Do you think it's OK to lie online? As you prepare your paragraph, think about the Unit Question, "Is it ever OK to lie?" and refer to the Self-Assessment checklist on page 160.

For alternative unit assignments, see the *Q: Skills for Success Teacher's Handbook*.

PLAN AND WRITE

A. BRAINSTORM Complete the activities.

1. Read the question from the website LiarsHelpGroup.com.

> **Chad Chat:** I spend a lot of time on the Internet. I go to many chat rooms and talk with many people online. I don't give my real name. I have an online name. Sometimes I also tell white lies about myself. It's fun. I feel like a different person. Is it OK to lie online?

2. Discuss these questions with a partner.
   a. Why do you think Chad Chat lies about himself online?
   b. Is it OK to lie about yourself online?

3. Discuss the reasons in the chart with your partner. Then write two new possible reasons.

Reasons it's OK to lie online	Reasons it's not OK to lie online
It doesn't hurt anyone.	*You can get in trouble.*

In Activity B, you have to say your opinion and give three reasons to **justify** it, or give support for it. **Justifying** your opinions helps people understand your ideas better.

B. PLAN Complete the outline. You can use ideas from Activity A or your own ideas.

Topic sentence: In my opinion, it (is / isn't) OK to lie online.

Reason 1: It (is / isn't) OK to lie online because ____________________

____

Reason 2: It (is / isn't) OK to lie online because ____________________

____

Reason 3: It (is / isn't) OK to lie online because ____________________

____

Concluding sentence: ____

____

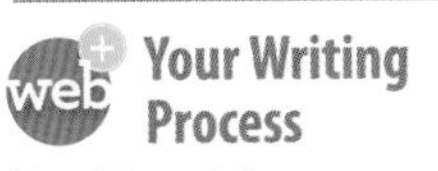

For this activity, you can look at Stage 1C, *Writing a First Draft*, in *Q Online Practice.*

C. WRITE Write your paragraph in your notebook. Look at the Self-Assessment checklist on page 160 to guide your writing.

REVISE AND EDIT

A. PEER REVIEW Read a partner's paragraph. Answer the questions and discuss them with your partner.

1. Is there a topic sentence? Write *TS* next to the topic sentence.
2. Are there three supporting reasons for your partner's opinion? Write *R* next to each reason.
3. Is there a concluding sentence? Write *CS* next to the concluding sentence.
4. Is there something you don't understand? Write a question mark (?) in the margin.

B. REWRITE Review the answers to the questions in Activity A. You may want to revise and rewrite your paragraph.

C. **EDIT** **Complete the Self-Assessment checklist as you prepare to write the final draft of your paragraph. Be prepared to hand in your work or discuss it in class.**

SELF-ASSESSMENT		
Yes	**No**	
☐	☐	Is the first line of the paragraph indented?
☐	☐	Does every sentence begin with a capital letter?
☐	☐	Does every sentence have final punctuation?
☐	☐	Does every sentence have a subject and a verb?
☐	☐	Does every subject and verb agree?
☐	☐	Is the spelling correct? Check a dictionary if you are not sure.
☐	☐	Does the paragraph have vocabulary words from the unit?
☐	☐	Are the infinitives of purpose correct?
☐	☐	Does the paragraph have a good concluding sentence?

Track Your Success

Circle the words you learned in this unit.

Nouns	Verbs
boss 🗝	admit 🗝
furniture 🗝	avoid 🗝
opinion 🗝	continue 🗝
punishment 🗝	control 🗝
purpose 🗝	fire 🗝
relationship 🗝	practice 🗝
reputation 🗝	require 🗝 AWL
trouble 🗝	respect 🗝
	trust 🗝

🗝 Oxford 2000 keywords

AWL Academic Word List

Check (✓) the skills you learned. If you need more work on a skill, refer to the page(s) in parentheses.

READING	○	I can identify pronoun referents. (p. 147)
VOCABULARY	○	I can recognize and use collocations. (p. 152)
WRITING	○	I can write concluding sentences. (p. 154)
GRAMMAR	○	I can recognize and use infinitives of purpose. (p. 156)
LEARNING OUTCOME	○	I can write a paragraph that explains my opinion about whether or not it is OK to lie in an online forum.

UNIT 9

Life Changes

READING ● marking the margins
VOCABULARY ● using the dictionary
GRAMMAR ● clauses with *after* and *after that*
WRITING ● making a timeline to plan your writing

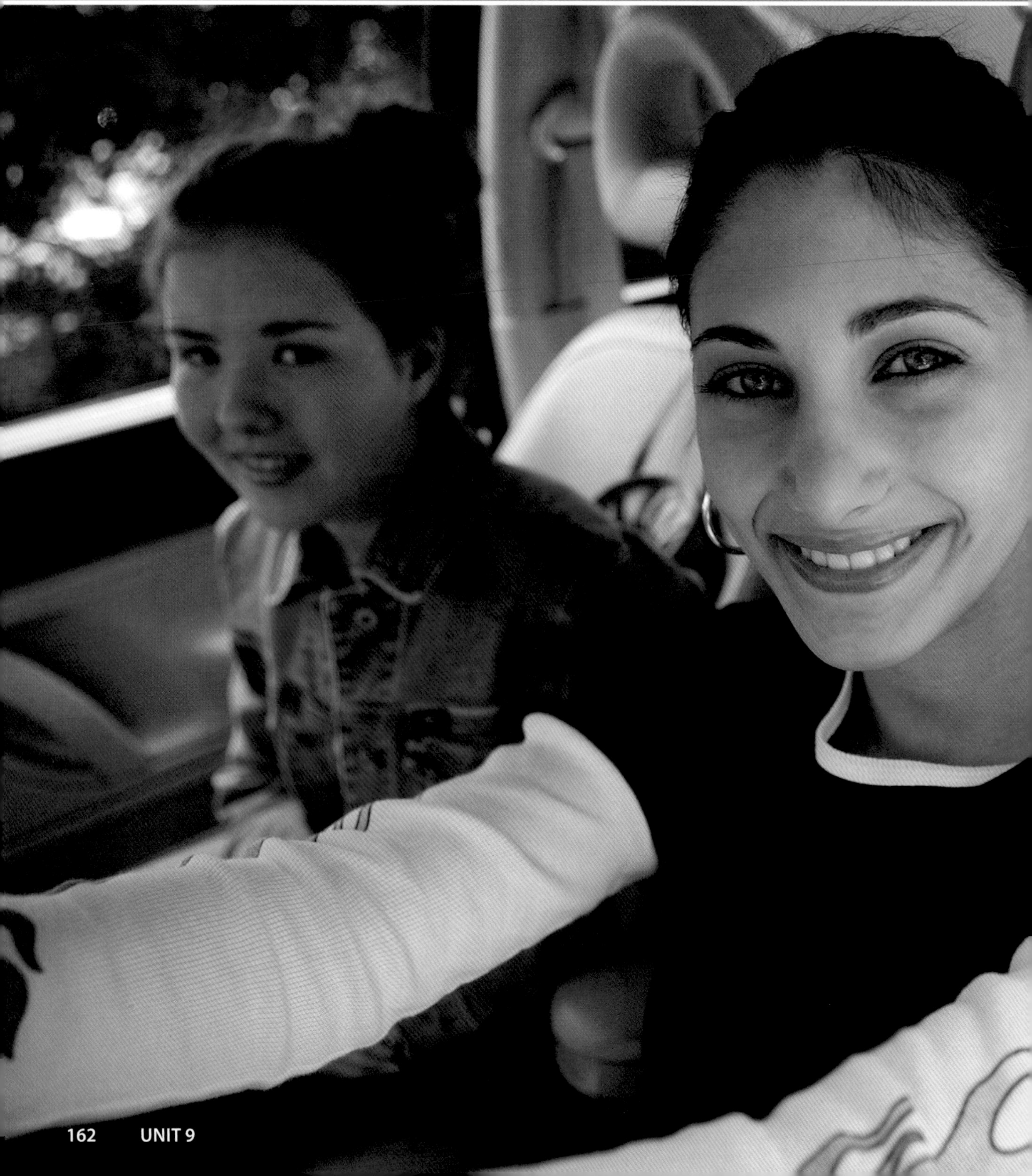

LEARNING OUTCOME

Describe events in your life that made you feel like an adult.

Unit QUESTION

How are children and adults different?

PREVIEW THE UNIT

A Discuss these questions with your classmates.

Are you an adult?

At what age does a person become an adult?

Look at the photo. What are the people doing? Are they adults or children?

B Discuss the Unit Question above with your classmates.

Listen to *The Q Classroom*, Track 11 on CD 2, to hear other answers.

C Work in a group. Complete the survey. Write *Y* (yes) or *N* (no) to record each answer. Then discuss the results with your group.

How do YOU define adult?

Are you an adult when you...?	Name	Name	Name	Total	
are 18 years old				Y=	N=
are 21 years old				Y=	N=
get married				Y=	N=
can drive a car				Y=	N=
own a home				Y=	N=
have a child				Y=	N=
earn money				Y=	N=
finish school				Y=	N=
leave your parents				Y=	N=
act like an adult				Y=	N=
(other)				Y=	N=
(other)				Y=	N=

D Discuss the photos with your group. Do any of the photos change your idea of an adult? Why or why not?

READING

READING 1 | What Is an Adult?

VOCABULARY

Here are some words from Reading 1. Read their definitions. Then complete each sentence.

define (*verb*) to say what a word means
grown (*adjective*) with the body of an adult; not a child
judgment (*noun*) your ability to make good decisions
legal (*adjective*) able to be done according to the laws of the government
organize (*verb*) to plan or arrange something
permission (*noun*) the action of giving someone the ability to do something
responsibility (*noun*) a duty to take care of someone or something
right (*noun*) what you can do, especially according to the law
vote (*verb*) to choose someone or something formally

1. Taking care of a child is a parent's ________________.
2. Use this chart. It will help you ________________ your ideas for writing.
3. Most children can't always make good choices because they don't have good ________________.
4. I'm 75 years old. All of my children are ________________.
5. In the United States, people ________________ for a president every four years.
6. In most countries, it isn't ________________ to get married at age 15.
7. You cannot leave the school without ________________ from a teacher.
8. What does the word *adult* mean? Can you please ________________ it?
9. All children have the ________________ to an education.

Reading Skill | Marking the margins 

Good readers think about the text as they read. They are active readers. One way to become an active reader is to **mark the margins**. The margins are the white space on each side of a text. Make marks in the margins when you find something interesting, when you read something you don't understand, and when you agree or disagree with the text.

Here are some marks you can use:

? = I don't understand.	✓ = I agree.
! = That's interesting!	✗ = I don't agree.

A. Read the paragraph. Then look at the marks the reader made and answer the questions.

Amish Teenagers

There is a group of people in the United States called the Amish. They believe in simple living and hard work. They don't use cars, TVs, or most
! kinds of technology. Amish children follow many rules, but when they turn 16, they are free to do whatever they want. They can leave their parents, drive cars, wear any clothes they want, and have big parties. This age is called
? *Rumspringa.* It ends when the teenagers make the decision between the outside world and the Amish world. The Amish
✓ believe their children need to make their own decisions. About 80 percent of Amish teenagers decide to return home and become Amish adults.

1. What does the reader not understand? ______________________
2. What does the reader think is interesting? ______________________
3. What does the reader agree with? ______________________

B. Mark the margins of Reading 1 as you read.

PREVIEW READING 1

This is an excerpt from a sociology textbook. It discusses what it means to be an adult.

Quickly skim the excerpt. Why do you think there is a picture of a human brain? Check (✓) your answer.

- ☐ to explain illnesses of the brain in teenagers
- ☐ to show the part of the brain that controls much adult thinking

CD 2 Track 12 **Read the excerpt.**

Vhat Is an Adult?

How do you know when a person is an adult? Does the person's age tell you? Or is an adult a person who takes on **responsibility** for work and family? There are different ways to **define** an adult.

ge

One way to define an adult is by age, but countries have very different ideas about the **legal** age of an adult. In India, a man can't marry without his parents' **permission** until age 21, and a woman can't marry until age 18. However, in Jordan, the legal ages are 16 for men and 15 for women. In Brazil, a 16-year-old can **vote**, but in most African nations, people don't have this **right** until they are 21. The legal driving age in Ethiopia is 14, and in Russia it is 18. The legal age of an adult is different around the world.

ody

Another way to define an adult is by the person's body. An adult is a person who is **grown** and can have children. This is a physical[1] definition of an adult. According to this definition, a 16-year-old is usually an adult.

Brain

4 Teenagers may have fully[2] grown bodies, but they don't usually think like adults. Their bodies usually stop growing at about age 17, but one part of the brain continues to grow until a person is about 25. This part of the brain, the frontal lobe, helps a person to understand cause and effect. It also helps a person to use good **judgment** to make decisions, solve problems, plan, and **organize**. When this part of the brain is fully grown at age 25, a person thinks like an adult.

Responsibilities

5 Another way of defining an adult is as a person who can take on important responsibilities like a job and a family. An adult respects others and understands that his or her own needs are not always the most important. This is the social[3]

[1] **physical:** relating to the body, not the mind
[2] **fully:** completely; totally
[3] **social:** connected with people who live in a place and the way they live together

definition of an adult. Some teenagers behave like adults, but most are not that responsible until they are over 20 years old.

What Is an Adult?

6 In conclusion, teenagers look like adults but are not yet adults. Some countries give teenagers the right to have adult responsibilities like marriage, voting, and driving, but teenagers don't always think or act like adults. Most people agree that after age 25, a person is an adult.

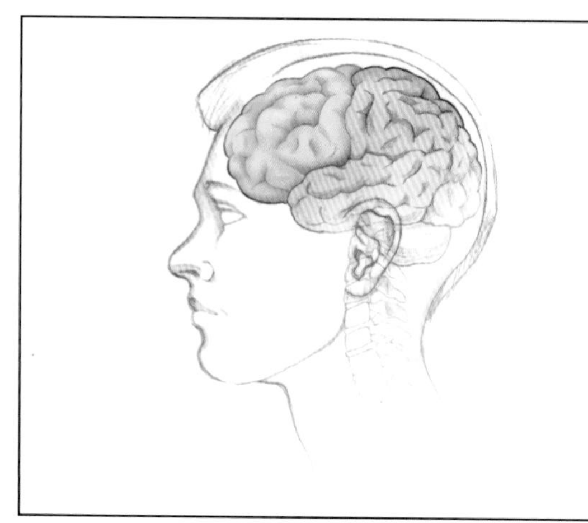

The frontal lo

MAIN IDEAS

Read the statements. Write *T* (true) or *F* (false).

____ 1. Countries have the same ideas about the legal age of adults.

____ 2. When a teenager's body stops growing, she or he is always an adult.

____ 3. Teenagers' brains continue to grow after their bodies have stopped growing.

____ 4. Teenagers with jobs and a family are adults according to one definition.

DETAILS

Circle the answer that best completes each statement.

1. A man in India can marry without his parents' permission when he is ______ years old.
   a. 16
   b. 18
   c. 21

2. People in Brazil can vote when they are ______.
   a. 16
   b. 18
   c. 21

3. People can get a driver's license in Ethiopia when they are ______ years old.
   a. 14
   b. 16
   c. 18

4. The human brain does not stop growing until a person is about ______ years old.
   a. 18
   b. 21
   c. 25

5. The last part of the brain to grow is the part that helps a person ______.
   a. be intelligent
   b. use good judgment
   c. learn languages

6. You can infer from the conclusion that ______.
   a. a person is an adult after age 25
   b. a person is an adult when his or her body is grown
   c. a person is an adult when she or he acts like an adult

WHAT DO YOU THINK?

Discuss the questions in a group. Then choose one question and write a paragraph about it in your notebook.

1. Which ideas in Reading 1 did you mark as interesting (!)? Why were they interesting?
2. Which ideas in Reading 1 did you agree (✓) or disagree (✗) with? Give reasons.
3. Which ideas do you not understand? Ask your classmates to explain them.

READING 2 | Becoming an Adult

VOCABULARY

Here are some words from Reading 2. Read the sentences. Then write each bold word next to the correct definition.

1. After the wedding, they had a big **celebration** with food, music, and dancing.
2. All the students like to **participate** in the class discussion. It's a noisy class.
3. On this map, the colors green and blue **represent** land and water.
4. The teachers in our school **collect** our homework every day. That's why I always have it ready.
5. The family lived in a small **village**, but then they moved to a big city.
6. My cat likes to **chase** birds, but he is too slow. The birds always fly away.
7. You usually **burn** wood when you make a fire.
8. Mike and Lisa got married in a quiet wedding **ceremony** in a garden.
9. The 100 years from 1901 through 2000 are called the 20th **century**.

a. ________________ (*verb*) to destroy something with fire

b. ________________ (*noun*) a time when you enjoy yourself because you have a special reason to be happy

c. ________________ (*noun*) a period of 100 years

d. ________________ (*verb*) to take things from different people or places and put them together

e. ________________ (*verb*) to do something together with other people

f. ________________ (*noun*) a formal public or religious event

g. ________________ (*noun*) a very small town

h. ________________ (*verb*) to run behind someone or something and try to catch it

i. ________________ (*verb*) to be an example or sign of something

PREVIEW READING 2

You are going to read postings on the *Across the World* magazine blog. The magazine asked readers to post stories from their countries.

Which country is each person from? Scan the blog and write the countries.

Astrid: ________________

Yasa: ________________

Min Joo: ________________

CD 2 Track 13 **Read the postings.**

Becoming an Adult

Home Log in

About

Links

Archives

January
February
March
April
May
June
July
August
September
October
November
December

Welcome to the *Across the World* blog!

FRIDAY, AUGUST 3 comments 0

1 *Across the World* magazine would like you to post your stories to our blog. What does becoming an adult mean in your country? Tell us your stories!

Becoming an adult in Norway

SUNDAY, AUGUST 5 comments 6

2 My name is Astrid, and I live in Norway. In my country, there is a **celebration** called *Russ* when students finish high school. I **participated** in the *Russ* celebration this year. It began on May 1 and ended on May 17. We wore clothes that **represented** our studies in school; for example, I wore red. All students who studied math wore red. We wore red clothes every day for 17 days. On the last day, we put on hats and walked in a parade[1]. At the end of the celebration, I was not a child anymore. I was an adult.

High school graduates in Norway enjoy their *Russ* celebration.

[1] **parade:** an event in which people, musical groups, cars, and trucks go down the street so that people can watch them

Becoming an adult in Papua New Guinea

MONDAY, AUGUST 6

comments 20

3 I am Yasa from Papua New Guinea. In my country, boys have a monthlong event called *Kovave*. When I was about to become a man, my uncles asked me to come into the forest to **collect** nuts with them. While I was walking in the forest, other men from the **village** surprised me and put a *Kovave* mask on my head. The *Kovave* mask represents spirits[2] in the forest. After the men put the mask on me, they **chased** me and some other boys with masks back to the village. For a month, the other boys and I wore the masks in the village. After a month, we had a big party with food and gifts. Then we went to the forest to **burn** our masks. After we returned to the village, we were men.

Boys in Papua New Guinea wear their *Kovave* masks.

Becoming an adult in Korea

WEDNESDAY, AUGUST 8

comments 36

4 I am from Korea. My name is Min Joo. I turned 19 years old this year, so I participated in my country's coming-of-age[3] **ceremony**. The ceremony started in the tenth **century**. At that time, the young prince[4] received new adult clothes to show that he was not a child anymore. This celebration became popular in the 14th century. In 1999, the government made the third Monday in May, Coming-of-Age Day. Now all 19-year-olds participate in the ceremony on that day. I wore a special Korean dress and walked with friends to the ceremony. My family gave me flowers and many gifts. Now I am an adult in Korea. I can drive, vote, and marry without my parents' permission.

On Coming-of-Age Day in Korea, men and women wear special Korean clothes.

[2] **spirit:** energy or life force
[3] **coming-of-age:** when a person becomes an adult
[4] **prince:** the son of a king or queen

MAIN IDEAS

Read the statements. Write *N* (Norway), *P* (Papua New Guinea), or *K* (Korea).

____ 1. People here have a *Russ* celebration.

____ 2. Only boys participate in the celebration in this country.

____ 3. There is a celebration called *Kovave* in this country.

____ 4. The celebration in this country is for 19-year-olds.

____ 5. The celebration here happens at the end of high school.

____ 6. The celebration here is called Coming-of-Age Day.

DETAILS

Circle the answer that best completes each statement.

1. The *Russ* celebration in Norway is ______ long.
   a. one week
   b. two weeks
   c. more than two weeks

2. The colors of clothes in the *Russ* celebration represent students' ______.
   a. studies
   b. hats
   c. teachers

3. In Papua New Guinea, boys go into the forest with ______ when they are ready to become men.
   a. their fathers
   b. their uncles
   c. their brothers

4. The boys' *Kovave* masks represent spirits of the ______.
   a. parents
   b. village
   c. forest

5. The first coming-of-age ceremony in Korea was in ______.
   a. the 10th century
   b. the 14th century
   c. the 20th century

6. A person becomes an adult in Korea at the age of ______________.
   a. 18
   b. 19
   c. 20

WHAT DO YOU THINK?

A. Discuss the questions in a group.

1. How do people in your country usually define *adult*?
2. Does your culture or one you know have a ceremony of some kind to celebrate becoming an adult? Explain it.

B. Think about both Reading 1 and Reading 2 as you discuss the questions.

1. Do you think some people become adults before others? Why or why not?
2. Which do you feel better defines an adult: a cultural ceremony or a person who stopped growing?

Vocabulary Skill Using the dictionary

Words in a dictionary sometimes have more than one definition. Each definition has a number. It is important to know which definition you need. Here are some tips for **finding the correct definition.**

- Read the complete sentence. Is the word a *noun*, *verb*, *adjective*, or *adverb*?
- Look at the context, or other words in the sentence. They can sometimes give you information about the word you don't know.

In the example below, you can see that Definition 1 is the best definition for the word *gift* because it is a gift one person gives to another. *Gift* can also mean ability, but none of the words in the sentence discuss ability, so Definition 2 does not make sense.

On his 18th birthday, he received a wonderful **gift** from his parents.

> **gift** /gɪft/ *noun* [*count*]
> **1** something that you give to or get from someone: *This week's magazine comes with a special* ***free gift****.* ➲ SYNONYM **present**
> **2** the natural ability to do something well: *She has a* ***gift for*** *languages.* ➲ SYNONYM **talent**

A. Read the sentences. Then write the number of the correct definition for each bold word.

> **col·lect**[1] /kəˈlɛkt/ *verb* (**col·lect, col·lect·ing, col·lect·ed**)
> **1** to take things from different people or places and put them together: *The teacher will collect the test booklets at the end of the exam.*
> **2** to bring together things that are the same in some way, in order to study or enjoy them: *My son collects stamps.*

___ 1. My brother **collects** toy cars. He has about 300 now.

___ 2. I **collected** all the library books in the house and returned them to the library.

re·spon·si·ble /rɪˈspɑnsəbl/ *adjective*
1 having the duty to take care of someone or something: *The driver is* ***responsible for*** *the lives of the people on the bus.*
2 being the person who made something bad happen: *Who was* ***responsible for*** *the accident?*
3 A **responsible** person is someone that you can trust: *We need a responsible person to take care of our son.* ⮌ **ANTONYM irresponsible**

____ 3. Kelly is very **responsible**. She's only 15, but she has a job, and she is saving money for college.

____ 4. I'm **responsible** for my younger brothers and sisters when we go to the park. I make sure they don't get hurt.

____ 5. Jack was **responsible** for the fire. He forgot the stove was on.

par·ty /ˈpɑrṭi/ *noun* [*count*] (*plural* **par·ties**)
1 a time when friends meet, usually in someone's home, to eat, drink, and enjoy themselves: *We're* ***having a party*** *this Saturday. Can you come?* • *a birthday party*
2 (**POLITICS**) a group of people who have the same ideas about politics: *He's a member of the Democratic Party.*

____ 6. Many people voted for the President's **party**.

____ 7. The children had a good time at the **party** with lots of games and food.

B. Look up each bold word in the dictionary. Find the correct definition and write it on the line. Pay attention to the part of speech.

1. Children need to learn the difference between **right** and wrong.

   right: ____

2. We sent the young man to **represent** our village at the meeting.

   represent: ____

3. The lawyer didn't agree with the **judgment**, but he did not say anything.

   judgment: ____

WRITING

Grammar Clauses with *after* and *after that* 

You can use *after* or *after that* when you write about a series of events. The word *after* makes it clear to the reader that one thing happened first and then another thing happened.

After

After combines two sentences into one. It comes before the first event. It can either begin the sentence or come in the middle of the sentence.

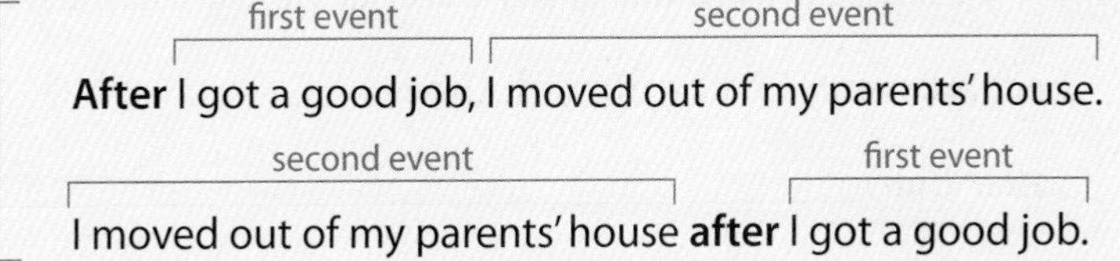

After that

Use *after that* to connect a second sentence to a first one. It comes in the second sentence and indicates a second event. It can come at the beginning or the end of the sentence.

first event | second event

I got my driver's license at 16. **After that**, I really felt like an adult.

first event | second event

I got my driver's license at 16. I really felt like an adult **after that**.

A. For each sentence or pair of sentences, circle the first event and underline the second event.

1. After (I turned 18), I graduated from high school.
2. I moved to New York after I finished college.
3. I had my first child when I was 25. After that, I wanted another child.
4. After the coming-of-age ceremony, my friends and I went to a party.
5. After I voted for the first time, I felt like a responsible adult.
6. I learned how to drive after I turned 18.

B. **Read the sentences. Write a sentence with *after* or two sentences with *after that.***

1. First event: We got married.

   Second event: My wife and I moved to California.

   (*after*) ______________________________

2. First event: I went to my coming-of-age ceremony.

   Second event: I still didn't feel like a real adult.

   (*after*) ______________________________

3. First event: I moved out of my parents' house when I was 19.

   Second event: I had a difficult time.

   (*after that*) ______________________________

4. First event: I turned 16 last year.

   Second event: I started being more responsible.

   (*after that*) ______________________________

Writing Skill | Making a timeline to plan your writing

A **timeline** is a list of important events and the times that they happened. You can make a timeline to help you write a narrative—a story.

Here is a timeline of someone's perfect day.

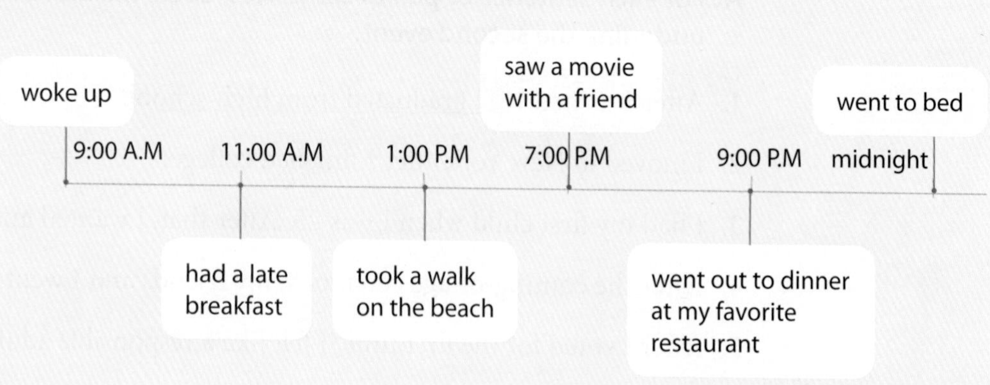

Here is a paragraph based on the timeline. Notice that you can add details to your paragraph that are not included in your timeline. Use your timeline only as a guide for your writing.

I had a perfect day off last Saturday. I woke up at 9:00 a.m. I read a book for a little while. Then I had a late breakfast at 11:00 a.m. At 1:00 p.m., I took a walk on the beach. It was a beautiful day. After that, I called a friend and invited her to dinner and a movie. At 7:00, I saw the movie with my friend, and at 9:00, we had dinner at my favorite restaurant. After dinner, I was really tired. I went to bed at midnight.

Tip Critical Thinking

Activity A asks you to **construct**, or make, a timeline about your perfect day. To make or construct something new, you have to put information together in a different way. This can help you understand your ideas better.

A. Make a timeline to show your perfect day in your notebook. Write a short note about each important event. Then tell a partner about your day.

B. Write at least six sentences about your perfect day in your notebook. Use your timeline, any other information you told your partner, and any other details you want to add.

Unit Assignment | Write one or two paragraphs about events in your life

In this assignment, you are going to write one or two paragraphs about events in your life that made you feel like an adult. As you prepare your paragraph(s), think about the Unit Question, "How are children and adults different?" and refer to the Self-Assessment checklist on page 180.

For alternative unit assignments, see the *Q: Skills for Success Teacher's Handbook*.

PLAN AND WRITE

A. BRAINSTORM Write a list of events in your life that made you feel like an adult. Write in your notebook for five minutes.

B. PLAN Complete the activities.

1. Choose four to six of the events you wrote about in Activity A. Put the events in order on a timeline in your notebook. (Draw a timeline like the one you made in Writing Skill, Activity A.)

2. Work with a partner. Tell your partner about the events on your timeline. Ask and answer questions about the events. Add any details to your timeline.

When you write your paragraph, remember to write two or three ideas that support your topic sentence and to write a concluding sentence.

C. WRITE Write one or two paragraphs in your notebook. Use the information from your timeline in Activity B to help you. You can use this topic sentence to begin your first paragraph, or write your own: *Several experiences in my life made me feel like an adult.* Look at the Self-Assessment checklist below to guide your writing.

Revise and Edit

A. PEER REVIEW Read a partner's paragraph(s). Answer the questions and discuss them with your partner.

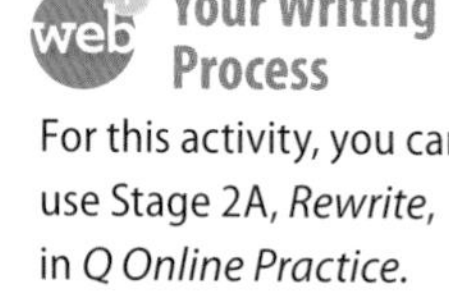

For this activity, you can use Stage 2A, *Rewrite,* in *Q Online Practice.*

1. Does each paragraph have a topic sentence? Write TS next to the topic sentence.
2. Are there supporting sentences? Write SS next to each supporting sentence.
3. Are there examples of *after* and *after that*? Are they correct?
4. Is there something you find especially interesting? Write an exclamation mark (!) in the margin.
5. Is there something you don't understand? Write a question mark (?) in the margin.

B. REWRITE Review the answers to the questions in Activity A. You may want to revise and rewrite your paragraph(s).

C. EDIT Complete the Self-Assessment checklist as you prepare to write the final draft of your paragraph. Be prepared to hand in your work or discuss it in class.

SELF-ASSESSMENT		
Yes	No	
☐	☐	Is the first line of each paragraph indented?
☐	☐	Does each sentence begin with a capital letter?
☐	☐	Does each sentence have final punctuation?
☐	☐	Does each sentence have a subject and a verb?
☐	☐	Does each subject and verb agree?
☐	☐	Is the spelling correct? Check a dictionary if you are not sure.
☐	☐	Does each paragraph have vocabulary words from the unit?
☐	☐	Is the use of *after* and *after that* correct?
☐	☐	Are there four to six events in the correct order?

Track Your Success

Circle the words you learned in this unit.

Nouns	Verbs	Adjectives
celebration	burn 🔑	grown
century 🔑	chase 🔑	legal 🔑 AWL
ceremony 🔑	collect 🔑	
judgment 🔑	define AWL	
permission 🔑	organize 🔑	
responsibility 🔑	participate AWL	
right 🔑	represent 🔑	
village 🔑	vote 🔑	

🔑 Oxford 2000 keywords

AWL Academic Word List

Check (✓) the skills you learned. If you need more work on a skill, refer to the page(s) in parentheses.

READING	I can mark the margins of a reading. (p. 166)
VOCABULARY	I can find the best definition when using the dictionary. (p. 175)
GRAMMAR	I can recognize and use clauses with *after* and *after that.* (p. 177)
WRITING	I can make a timeline to plan my writing. (p. 178)
LEARNING OUTCOME	I can describe events in my life that made me feel like I was an adult.

UNIT 10

Fear

READING ● identifying facts and opinions
VOCABULARY ● word families
WRITING ● contrasting ideas with *however*
GRAMMAR ● comparative adjectives

LEARNING OUTCOME

Describe an unreasonable fear and explain how it can be avoided.

Unit QUESTION

What are you afraid of?

PREVIEW THE UNIT

A **Discuss these questions with your classmates.**

Do you easily become afraid?

What do you do to stay safe?

Look at the photo. Are you afraid of spiders?

B **Discuss the Unit Question above with your classmates.**

Listen to *The Q Classroom*, Track 14 on CD 2, to hear other answers.

C **For each statement, mark an ✗ on the line according to how you feel. Then compare your answers in a group.**

	Strongly disagree ⟷ Strongly agree
1. The world is a dangerous place.	⟷
2. I am afraid to walk alone at night.	⟷
3. I never talk to people I don't know.	⟷
4. There are many dangerous people in the world.	⟷
5. I wash my hands a lot so I don't get sick.	⟷
6. The news on TV is scary.	⟷

D **Look at the photos. How does each photo make you feel? Write a sentence about each photo in your notebook. Then discuss the questions below with your group.**

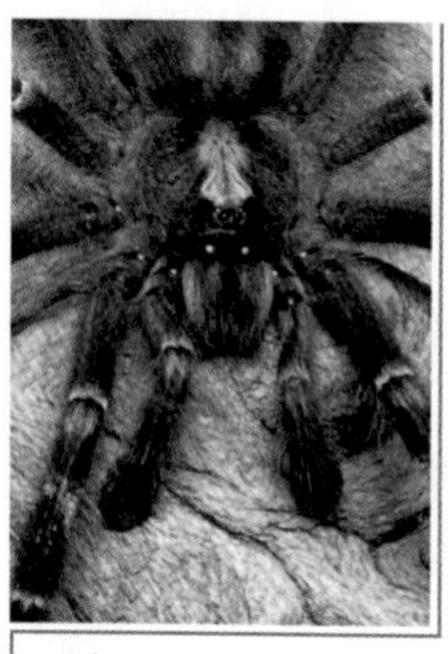
spiders

snakes

dogs

heights

1. Did you and other members of your group write similar ideas?
2. Which photo do you fear the most? Why?
3. Which photo do you fear the least? Why?

READING 1 | A Dangerous World?

VOCABULARY

Tip for Success

The words *affect* and *effect* are sometimes confused. *Affect* (verb) means to change. *Effect* (noun) means the change that happens because of something. For example: Crime *affects* us. The *effects* are fear and worry.

Here are some words from Reading 1. Read the sentences. Then write each bold word next to the correct definition.

1. This neighborhood has a lot of **crime**. Be careful!
2. I don't like **violent** movies. I don't like to see people get hurt.
3. Every day, there are many important news events in the world. However, our **focus** is often on movie stars or other famous people
4. We saw a **scary** movie last night. I was so afraid I couldn't sleep!
5. News websites usually **report** on news events more quickly than newspapers or TV news.
6. Cats are very **common** in this country. Many families own one.
7. Smoking can **affect** your health. It can make you sick.
8. Most people agree that eating a lot of fast food can have a **negative** effect on your health.

a. ________________ (*adjective*) bad; not positive or good

b. ________________ (*adjective*) making you feel afraid

c. ________________ (*noun*) something that someone does that is against the law

d. ________________ (*noun*) the center of attention or interest

e. ________________ (*adjective*) strong and dangerous; can hurt you

f. ________________ (*adjective*) happening often or found in many places

g. ________________ (*verb*) to make something or someone change in a particular way, especially in a bad way

h. ________________ (*verb*) to give people information about something that happened

PREVIEW READING 1

This is a magazine article that discusses interesting facts about crime and crime reporting over the past 15 years.

Skim the chart. What does it tell you about crime from 1992 to 2007? Check (✓) your answer.

☐ It's gone up. ☐ It's gone down.

CD 2 Track 15 **Read the article.**

A Dangerous World?

1 Is **crime** increasing in your town or city? In many places, crime rates are going down. The truth is that crime rates are much lower today than 50 years ago. However, most people believe that crime rates are increasing. They think that **violent** crime happens in their towns and cities all the time.

What makes people afraid?

2 Any day of the week, you can turn on the television and see a crime drama[1]. The first story on the evening news is usually a story about violent crime. On some news shows, over 40 percent of the news stories are about crime. Why is there such a **focus** on crime? It is because **scary** shows and news programs are popular.

Does TV give people a true picture of the world?

3 No. Television does not give people a true idea of the level of danger in the world. Here is an interesting example. Between 1992 and 2007, the rate of violent crime went down in Canada. However, a study showed that during that time, news stories about violent crime increased from 10 to 25 percent. One year, almost 25 percent of the stories the Canadian news **reported** were about gun crime, but only 3.3 percent of violent crime that year was gun crime.

Violent Crimes in Canada, 1962 to 2007

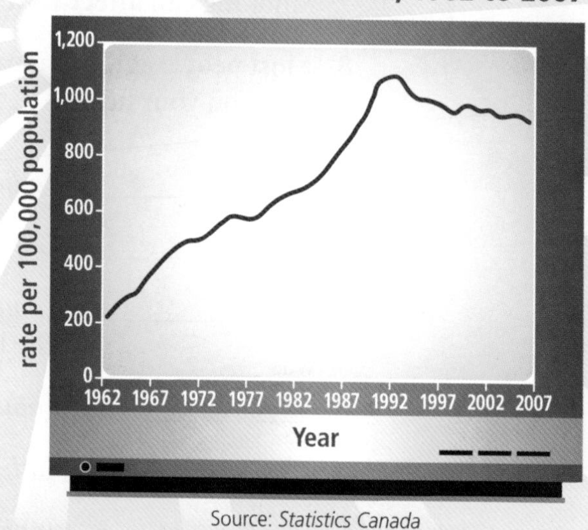

Source: *Statistics Canada*

Television's focus on crime gives people the wrong idea. People believe there is more crime than there really is. They think violent crime is **common**.

[1] **drama:** a play for the theater, radio, or television

What are the effects of this exaggerated[2] focus on violent crime?

4 It **affects** people's lives in a **negative** way. This focus on violent crime results in increased feelings of fear. In order to protect themselves, some people avoid going out. They do not talk to their neighbors. As a result, they know and trust fewer people. They have fewer friends. This increases their fear about the dangers in the world.

5 Fear of crime can also affect people's health. Many parents keep their children inside their homes. They believe the world outside is too dangerous. The children watch more television and don't walk, run, or play sports outside. They become less healthy. This is true for older adults too.

6 Television's focus on crime makes us believe the world is a scarier place than it is. It makes us lonelier and less happy and healthy. Facts show that we should learn to worry less. It's good to be careful and stay safe, but the world around us is actually safer than we think.

[2] **exaggerated:** bigger or worse than it really is

MAIN IDEAS

Circle the answer that best completes each statement according to Reading 1.

1. The crime rate is ______ in many places.
   a. going up
   b. going down
2. Most people think the crime rate is ______.
   a. going up
   b. going down
3. Canadian television news made people believe that the crime rate was ______.
   a. going up
   b. going down
4. Television's focus on crime affects people ______.
   a. in positive ways
   b. in negative ways

DETAILS

Circle the answer that best completes each statement according to Reading 1.

1. On some news shows, _______ of the stories are about crime.
   a. more than 50 percent
   b. more than 40 percent
   c. about 54 percent
2. News stations report stories about crime because _______.
   a. the news stories are popular
   b. the news stories make us afraid
   c. there is no other news
3. Between 1992 and 2007, _______ in Canada increased from about 10 to 25 percent.
   a. violent crime
   b. stories about violent crime
   c. gun crime
4. The article does NOT say that television's focus on crime affects _______.
   a. people's ideas of the world
   b. health
   c. marriage rates
5. Fear of crime can affect children's health because they _______.
   a. stay inside and don't play sports
   b. feel nervous all the time
   c. eat more in order to feel safe

WHAT DO YOU THINK?

Discuss the questions in a group. Then choose one question and write two or three sentences about it in your notebook.

1. Do you watch the news on TV? Do you read the news online or in a newspaper? Tell your group where you get the news and why (or why you don't get the news).
2. Do you think crime is going up or going down where you live? Explain your answer.
3. Are there differences in opinion between group members who watch the news on TV and those who read the news? Is the reason similar to what the article says: People believe there is more crime than there really is?

Reading Skill Identifying facts and opinions 

A supporting sentence or detail in a text is usually either a **fact** or an **opinion**. Knowing the difference between a fact and an opinion is important for a reader. It can help you decide the purpose of a text and judge how well the author supports the ideas in the text.

Facts are things that you know happened or are true. Opinions are what you think or feel about something.

Here are some common words that tell you a statement is an opinion and not a fact.

- The verbs *think* and *believe*.

  I **think** violent movies are scary.
  Some people **believe** violent movies cause more crime.

- The helping verb *should*. (*Should* goes before another verb. You use *should* to tell someone what you think is or isn't a good idea.)

  Television news **should** report more positive news.
  Reporters **shouldn't** focus only on crime.

A. Read each pair of sentences. Write *F* (fact) or *O* (opinion).

1. ___ a. In Canada, crime rates are going down.
   ___ b. People believe crime rates are increasing.
2. ___ a. I think the streets are dangerous at night.
   ___ b. There was a robbery on Jackson Street last night.
3. ___ a. Children shouldn't watch violent programs on television.
   ___ b. By the age of 18, people see 200,000 violent crimes on television.
4. ___ a. Many studies show that violent news stories affect people in a negative way.
   ___ b. Some people believe that violent stories on the news make us more afraid.

B. Read Reading 1 again. Underline all the statements of opinion that use the words *think, believe,* and *should.*

READING 2 | Can We Trust Our Fears?

VOCABULARY

Here are some words from Reading 2. Read their definitions. Then complete each sentence.

contain (*verb*) to have something inside
death (*noun*) when a life finishes
disease (*noun*) an illness or sickness
factor (*noun*) one of the things that can affect or change a decision, or a situation
fat (*noun*) an oil we get from the plants, seeds, and animals we eat
frighten (*verb*) to make someone feel afraid
harm (*verb*) to hurt or damage someone or something
pleasure (*noun*) the feeling of being happy or enjoying something
reasonable (*adjective*) fair or right in a particular situation

1. My horse is big and strong, but he never tries to ________________ anyone.
2. Stress is one ________________ that can affect your health. Food is another.
3. I was sorry to hear about the ________________ of your father. He was a wonderful man.
4. That's a ________________ plan. I'm sure it will work out well.
5. Scary movies really ________________ me!
6. The white part of the meat is ________________. I cut it off and don't eat it because it's not healthy.
7. My neighbor has a serious ________________. He is in the hospital.
8. I love to go to nice restaurants. Eating there is a great ________________ for me.
9. Our bodies ________________ a lot of water—over 50 percent, in fact, is water.

PREVIEW READING 2

This is an online article about common fears and how these fears often don't make any sense. Which are you more afraid of: riding in a car or riding on an airplane? Discuss your answer with your classmates.

CD 2 Track 16 **Read the article.**

Can We Trust Our Fears?

1 Are you more afraid of bird flu[1] or the common flu[2]? Which **frightens** you more, mad cow **disease**[3] or heart disease[4]? Fear is a natural human feeling. The purpose of fear is to protect us from things that **harm** us. However, we can't always trust our fears.

2 Sometimes we are afraid of things that are not likely to happen. Many people think bird flu is very dangerous, but we don't worry about the common flu. Only 256 people died of the bird flu between 2003 and 2009. However, every year 250,000 to 500,000 people die from the common flu. Many people are not afraid to eat unhealthy foods, but we're afraid of getting mad cow disease from beef. In fact, we are much more likely to get heart disease than mad cow disease. Heart disease is the number-one cause of **death** in the world. In 2005 alone, 17.5 million people died of heart disease. Fewer than 300 people, however, ever died of mad cow disease. Why are we more afraid of things that are not really dangerous? There are a few different **factors**.

We are more likely to get heart disease than mad cow disease.

3 First of all, when something is familiar to us or common in our experience, we fear it less. For example, most of us get the common flu several times in our lives. However, we never get bird flu. We probably don't know anyone who had bird flu. Bird flu is unknown, so it's scarier.

[1] **bird flu:** an illness humans can get from birds
[2] **common flu:** an illness many people get every year
[3] **mad cow disease:** an illness that kills cows and can kill people who eat beef from sick cows
[4] **heart disease:** any disease that causes the heart to stop working correctly

4 Another factor is control. We are more afraid of things we cannot control. Mad cow disease is dangerous. It is very difficult to know if meat **contains** mad cow disease. Mad cow disease cannot be stopped by doctors. We have no control over it. Doctors can usually help people with heart disease, though. They can control it. And doctors believe people can fight heart disease. They say that we should exercise and eat less of some kinds of **fat**. We know we can control heart disease.

5 A third possible factor is **pleasure**. If something gives us pleasure, we might continue to do it despite[5] the danger. For example, maybe your mother and your grandfather had heart disease. You know that you need to eat well, but you really like food with a lot of fat. So you eat it anyway. You say, "Someday I will change the way I eat, but I'm hungry and the unhealthy food is delicious."

6 Now, think about the things that you are afraid of. How likely are they to happen? Do you think your fears are **reasonable**? Think about your fears honestly, and you might be surprised. You may find out that you are living with unnecessary fears.

[5] **despite:** although something happened or is true

MAIN IDEAS

A. Circle the answer that best completes each statement according to Reading 2.

1. Things that are ______ frighten us more.
   a. familiar
   b. unfamiliar
2. We often fear things that we have ______ over.
   a. no control
   b. complete control
3. Our fears are ______.
   a. usually right
   b. sometimes wrong
4. We often do things that may hurt us because we ______.
   a. enjoy them
   b. don't believe they are bad

DETAILS

A. Are these statements true or false according to Reading 2? Write *T* (true) or *F* (false).

___ 1. Heart disease is the number-one cause of death in the world.

___ 2. From 2003 to 2009, bird flu killed 256 people.

___ 3. Every year, up to half a million people die from the common flu.

___ 4. More than 17 million people died of mad cow disease in 2005.

___ 5. Bird flu is less familiar than the common flu.

___ 6. We are usually afraid of things that we know well.

B. Reading 2 discusses both facts about people and people's opinions. Scan the reading to find two more facts about people and two more opinions that people have about illness and fear.

Facts

1. Every year, 250,000 to 500,000 people die from the common flu.
2. ______________________________
3. ______________________________

Opinions

1. Many people think bird flu is very dangerous.
2. ______________________________
3. ______________________________

WHAT DO YOU THINK?

A. Discuss the questions in a group.

1. What are you afraid of? List four things in your notebook. Then read your list to your group. Do you and other members of your group have similar fears?
2. Are your fears things that are unknown? Are they things you have no control over? Are you afraid of things that are not likely to happen?

3. Choose one reasonable fear and one unreasonable fear from Steps 1 and 2. Write about each kind of fear.

   A reasonable fear: ________________

   Why is it reasonable? (Explain the danger.) ________________________

   ____

   An unreasonable fear: ______________________________________

   Why is it unreasonable? ____________________________________

   ____

   Why are you afraid of it anyway? ____________________________

B. Think about both Reading 1 and Reading 2 as you discuss the questions.

1. In Reading 1 and Reading 2, you read that people sometimes fear things unnecessarily. What do you think people *should* be afraid of?
2. Which fears do you think are unreasonable? Explain your answer.

Vocabulary Skill | Word families

web

A **word family** is a group of words that come from the same word. The bold words in the sentences are members of the same word family. Notice that they are each a different part of speech.

Some people spend a lot of money on home **protection.** (noun)
They want to **protect** their homes from criminals. (verb)
They buy **protective** alarm systems for their homes. (adjective)

This chart shows two word families.

Noun	Verb	Adjective	Adverb
familiarity	**familiarize**	**familiar**	**familiarly**
pleasure	**please**	**pleasant**	**pleasantly**

When you learn a new word, also try to learn the other members of the word family. Learning word families can help build your vocabulary more quickly.

A. **Complete the chart. Use your dictionary to help you.**

	Noun	Verb	Adjective	Adverb
1.	*fear*	*fear*	*fearful*	*fearfully*
2.	violence			
3.			believable	
4.		endanger		
5.			harmful	
6.	safety			

B. **Complete each sentence with a word from the chart in Activity A.**

1. We often ________________ the things we can't control.
2. We feel ________________ in this neighborhood. We often go out at night to visit our neighbors.
3. The man hit the wall ________________. He was very angry.
4. The news reports a lot of gun ________________, but most crime isn't gun crime.
5. You may be in ________________ if you travel alone at night.
6. I'm not afraid when Susan drives because she drives very ________________.
7. Being afraid of the dark is a common ________________.

WRITING

Writing Skill | Contrasting ideas with *however*

The word *however* introduces an idea that is different from the idea in the sentence before it. It contrasts with the idea before it. *However* is similar in meaning to the word *but*.

My neighborhood is dangerous, **but** it has many nice qualities.
My neighborhood is dangerous. **However**, it has many nice qualities.

But is a *conjunction*. It connects two sentences into one. *However* is a *transition*. It links a sentence to the one before it.

- *However* usually comes at the beginning of the second sentence. Use a comma after *however*.

Crime rates are going down. **However**, most people think there is more crime.

- When you want the focus of the sentence to be about the subject, you can put *however* after the subject. Put commas before and after it.

Crime rates are going down. Most people, **however**, think the world is more dangerous.

- When the contrast is less important, you can also put *however* at the end of the sentence. Place a comma before it.

Crime rates are going down. Most people think there is more crime, **however**.

A. Connect the sentences with *but* and *however.* Pay attention to punctuation (commas and periods).

1. Violent crime frightens us.
   We are more likely to die in a car.

   a. *Violent crime frightens us, but we are more likely to die in a car.*

   b. *Violent crime frightens us. However, we are more likely to die in a car.*

2. We like to watch violent TV shows.
   Violence makes us anxious.

   a. ______________________________

   b. ______________________________

3. I am more likely to die in a car accident.
   I fear an airplane crash more.

   a. ______________________________

   b. ______________________________

4. Women fear crime more than men.
   Crime happens more often to men.

   a. ______________________________

   b. ______________________________

5. Most crimes are not violent.
   Television focuses on the unusual and violent crimes.

   a. ______________________________

   b. ______________________________

B. Rewrite the sentences from Activity A with *however.* This time, write *however* in a different place in the sentence.

1. ______________________________
2. ______________________________
3. ______________________________
4. ______________________________
5. ______________________________

Grammar | Comparative adjectives 

We use **comparative adjectives** to compare two people, places, things, or ideas.

Crime is **high** in my neighborhood. → Crime is **higher** in yours.
I'm **afraid** of getting the flu. → My sister is **more afraid**.

Here are some rules to help you form comparative adjectives correctly.

- Add *-er* to one-syllable adjectives. (A *syllable* is a part of a word with a vowel sound. One-syllable words have one vowel sound.) Add *-r* when the adjective ends in *-e*.

high → **higher** late → **later**

- When the one-syllable adjective ends in consonant + vowel + consonant, double the last consonant and add *-er*.

big → **bigger** hot → **hotter**

- Do not double the consonant when the adjective ends in *-w*, *-x*, or *-y*.

low → **lower** gray → **grayer**

- For two-syllable adjectives that end in -y, drop the *-y* and add *-ier*.

scary → scar**ier** crazy → craz**ier**

- For most other adjectives with two or more syllables, use *more* + adjective.

fearful → **more** fearful frightening → **more** frightening

- Use comparative adjective + *than* in sentences comparing two things.

My neighborhood is **safer than** your neighborhood.
Your neighborhood is **more dangerous than** my neighborhood.

Note: The words *good* and *bad* are irregular.

good → **better** bad → **worse**

A. Complete the chart with the comparative form of each adjective.

Adjective	Comparative Adjective
1. afraid	*more afraid*
2. big	
3. careful	
4. dangerous	
5. easy	
6. new	
7. reasonable	
8. safe	
9. smart	
10. violent	

B. Write sentences using the words and phrases. Use the comparative forms of the adjectives and *than*.

1. heart disease / mad cow disease / common

   Heart disease is more common than mad cow disease.

2. I believe / flying / driving / dangerous

   ____

3. I think / crime dramas / scary / real life

   ____

4. the crime rate in Canada in 2007 / the crime rate in Canada 15 years before / low

   ____

Unit Assignment | Write one or more paragraphs about an unreasonable fear

In this assignment, you are going to write one or more paragraphs about an unreasonable fear that you have or that you know about. Why is it unreasonable and how can you avoid the fear? As you prepare your paragraph(s), think about the Unit Question, "What are you afraid of?" and refer to the Self-Assessment checklist on page 202.

For alternative unit assignments, see the *Q: Skills for Success Teacher's Handbook*.

PLAN AND WRITE

A. BRAINSTORM Think of fears that you feel are unreasonable. Write four fears in the chart. Then tell why they are unreasonable.

Fear		Why It's Unreasonable
flying on an airplane	→	only 1 in 11 million chance of dying in a plane crash
	→	
	→	
	→	

Critical Thinking

Activity B helps you **develop** your ideas before you write. **Developing** your ideas lets you think them through and make them more complete. This will make your writing stronger.

B. PLAN Choose one fear from your chart in Activity A. Complete the activities. Write in your notebook.

1. Write a topic sentence. Use this sentence or write your own:

   ________________________ is an unreasonable fear because

   ________________________.

2. Explain the fear you chose and why you or people fear it.
3. Tell why it is unreasonable and how you can avoid that fear.
4. Write a concluding sentence.

C. WRITE Write your paragraph(s). Look at the Self-Assessment checklist on page 202 to guide your writing.

REVISE AND EDIT

Your Writing Process

For this activity, you could also use Stage 2A, *Peer Review* in *Q Online Practice*.

A. PEER REVIEW Read a partner's paragraph(s). Answer the questions and discuss them with your partner.

1. Does each paragraph have a topic sentence? Write TS next to the topic sentences.
2. Are there supporting sentences? Write SS next to each supporting sentence.
3. Did the writer explain the fear?
4. Did the writer explain why the fear is unreasonable?
5. Is there something you don't understand? Write a question mark (?) in the margin.

B. REWRITE Review the answers to the questions in Activity A. You may want to revise and rewrite your paragraph(s).

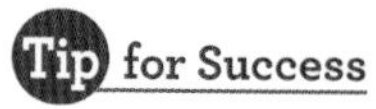

When you revise your writing, look for ways to make your sentences shorter. Try to cut out any extra words or unnecessary information. Keep only the important information.

C. EDIT Complete the Self-Assessment checklist as you prepare to write the final draft of your paragraph(s). Be prepared to hand in your work or discuss it in class.

SELF-ASSESSMENT		
Yes	No	
☐	☐	Is the first line of each paragraph indented?
☐	☐	Does every sentence begin with a capital letter?
☐	☐	Does every sentence have final punctuation?
☐	☐	Does every sentence have a subject and a verb?
☐	☐	Does every subject and verb agree?
☐	☐	Is the spelling correct? Check a dictionary if you are not sure.
☐	☐	Does the paragraph have vocabulary words from the unit?
☐	☐	Are the comparative adjectives correct?
☐	☐	Is the use of *however* correct?

Track Your Success

Circle the words you learned in this unit.

Nouns	**Verbs**	**Adjectives**
crime 🔑	affect 🔑 AWL	common 🔑
death 🔑	contain 🔑	negative 🔑 AWL
disease 🔑	frighten 🔑	reasonable 🔑
factor AWL	harm 🔑	scary
fat 🔑	report 🔑	violent 🔑
focus AWL		
pleasure 🔑		

🔑 Oxford 2000 keywords

AWL Academic Word List

Check (✓) the skills you learned. If you need more work on a skill, refer to the page(s) in parentheses.

READING	○	I can identify facts and opinions. (p. 189)
VOCABULARY	○	I can recognize and use word families. (p. 194)
WRITING	○	I can contrast ideas with *however.* (p. 196)
GRAMMAR	○	I can recognize and use comparative adjectives. (p. 198)
LEARNING OUTCOME	●	I can describe an unreasonable fear and explain how it can be avoided.